Overcoming Depression

Overcoming Depression

by
PAUL A. HAUCK

THE WESTMINSTER PRESS
Philadelphia

Published by The Westminster Press ®
Philadelphia, Pennsylvania

PRINTED IN THE UNITED STATES OF AMERICA

10   9

Library of Congress Cataloging in Publication Data

Hauck, Paul A.
  Overcoming depression.

  1. Depression, Mental. 2. Rational-emotive psychotherapy. I. Title.
  RC537.H37   616.8'95   72-13416
  ISBN 0-664-24969-8

To the most creative thinker I have ever met:

ALBERT ELLIS

Contents

Preface   11

1. How May I Help You?   *13*

2. Bad Me!   *27*

3. Be Kind to Yourself   *57*

4. Poor Me!   *77*

5. Poor You!   *107*

6. Some Final Advice   *129*

Preface

DEPRESSION IS NOT THE MOST COMMON EMOTIONAL DIS-
turbance. Anger and fear are. However, people do not
seek help for these two afflictions as often as they do for
feelings of guilt, despair, and depression. This is probably
because the latter are recognized as the types of disturbances with which psychotherapists often work,
whereas getting mad or worried is thought to be normal.

Unfortunately, too little has been understood about
depression until now. The poor soul who hated himself,
lived a life feeling inferior, or felt life wasn't worth the
effort was routinely medicated, sometimes shocked (without understanding how he became depressed), and was
offered psychoanalysis, or some variety thereof, as the
psychotherapeutic method of choice.

That time is past. It is now possible, with new methods,
for the depressed individual to learn how to get over
this pain, practically forever. Even better news is the
fact that this often can be done in a short time if the
right counseling techniques are used. This is what I have
tried to show in this book: how people make themselves
depressed, how they keep that depression alive, and how
they can prevent depression in the future.

11

This book is written for you, the layman who does not know the technical psychological terms most books on this subject use. I have written in an easygoing style with numerous examples to help explain the points I am trying to make. Anyone with a reasonable desire and an average skill in reading should be able to understand what I have to say and can most certainly use this knowledge to fight his depression. Some of you will benefit greatly, I think, even to the point where you can correct your disturbance almost completely. Others of you will get a good start in overcoming your depressive moods but may need professional counseling to complete the job.

Should you not need great help yourself, but someone whom you care for does, consider this book a good source of advice. You can help your mate, parents, children, or friends to overcome depression by telling them what you have learned, how you have profited from studying this book, and how others have changed their lives after they understood the three reasons for depression.

If I have accomplished these goals, I will be more than satisfied. So read on! There is hope for you. The material in this book has come from the lives of my clients who were just as depressed as you. They were helped. You will be helped too!

P.A.H.

1

How May I Help You?

WHEN I WAS ONLY BRIEFLY OUT OF GRADUATE SCHOOL, I worked in a community mental health center. Practically every person with whom I counseled had uncomfortable mood swings which sometimes went from a low mood back up to normal, or went from a high mood back down to normal. My most baffling client, however, was the one whose mood hit bottom and stayed there.

For a brand-new clinical psychologist this was a most frustrating challenge. The girl I am referring to was bright, well educated, and came from a secure financial background. She had several children but was divorced. She lived in her own home, had no real money worries, and should have been no more depressed than any number of thousands of others whose lives are really not that bad. For these reasons I found it hard to imagine what in the world she was so down about and why she couldn't find a reason to smile.

Be that as it may, Ruth (not her real name) had had a long history of getting depressed. She was now in her mid-twenties and had had depressive episodes since early adolescence. She had been hospitalized about two or three times, as I remember, had been tranquilized and energized for months at a time, had electroshock therapy,

13

and was a frequent visitor to the mental health center, where practically every staff person had seen her in counseling.

I was able to do nothing for her during the first weeks of counseling. If anything, she became somewhat more depressed, more dependent, and more sure that she would never come out of this current depressive mood. And guess what? She was beginning to convince me that she was right! Whatever it was I was doing sure wasn't making history. I listened to her very sympathetically for hours at a time. I analyzed her dreams as I had learned to do according to the revered teachings of the great Sigmund Freud. I took her back into her childhood and attempted to reconstruct her life to see where it had gone sour. In short, I did everything I had been taught to do, but it wasn't doing her or me any good. Instead, she wept more when she could see I was becoming unsure of myself. She then began calling me each morning before I left for the office to let me know that she could barely get started that day and please couldn't I do or say something that would give her the courage to go on. When she reached the stage where she couldn't sign and address her Christmas cards and when her mother had to go over to her home to fix lunch and dinner for Ruth and her children, I felt that it was time to look at my methods very closely and make any changes my common sense suggested.

My psychoanalytic training warned me against working with persons other than the client. That was why I did not follow my natural inclination to encourage Ruth's mother to let her alone. It was fairly obvious to me that the well-meaning mother was doing so much for the daughter whenever things got a little tough that Ruth never really faced trial and error by herself. Before she could pull herself together when she goofed off, her mother was there Johnny-on-the-spot to take all the responsibilities off Ruth's shoulders. My client was relieved to have the help, of course, but then she felt inferior that she needed the help and guilty that she accepted it.

At this stage of my professional growth, it never occurred to me to talk Ruth out of feeling guilty for playing the role of a helpless child. Instead, I thought I might make a break in the neurosis by getting the mother to leave her daughter alone. I called the mother in for a consultation and firmly advised her to visit her daughter no more than once every several days, not to call her each day, and not to bring over baked goods or to invite Ruth and the children to her home for supper.

Fortunately she accepted my advice and understood fully what I was trying to achieve. It scared her somewhat to think what would happen to her weak and inadequate daughter if she couldn't rely on someone stronger, but she took my counsel literally and stayed away.

Ruth had a worse time of it for a while, but because no one would do for her she began doing for herself. I encouraged her to handle her affairs the best she could, not to expect too much of herself, and to consider any little success a positive gain. If she would work at her own speed, I was certain that she could get her confidence back even if it took months. I found myself talking common sense to her rather than keeping quiet as I was psychoanalytically supposed to do. I gave advice until it was coming out of my ears. But she listened, debated over my suggestions, went home and tried some of my advice, and reported to me the following week.

In a matter of a few weeks she was not calling me every morning, she was handling her housework and the children, and her mood was definitely lifting. In short, before a half year passed she was out of the woods and her old self again.

I was so curious and pleased by this progress that I decided to write a paper for an upcoming institute given by the local mental health professionals. In the paper I tried to analyze why Ruth had improved and I hazarded the guess that she would probably not have any depressions again if she followed the habits she had been following during the previous months. Looking back on this analysis, I can see how incomplete my understanding was then and how much more quickly she could have gained improvement. I did not then know how to deal with guilt and self-pity—her two worst problems—and as a result I dealt with them only tangentially. Happily it was enough, but in another case it could just as easily not have been.

At the mental health institute where I delivered the paper on Ruth's recovery I was roundly criticized for suggesting that I had made a permanent change in the client. One of the most respected professionals attending the institute said kind words about how I had brought Ruth back to full functioning again but cautioned me not to be overly optimistic about her chances of remaining undepressed. Everyone knew that depression is largely a physical problem and that it runs in a cycle. Ruth had lived through a number of cycles already and would surely go through others.

That was about twenty years ago. Ruth has had only one serious depressive episode during all those intervening years. She has gone on to college and been working and supporting herself nicely all the while. As proof of her improvement I have received a Christmas gift each year for the past twenty years from the ex-depressive who just signs her name "Ruth."

A New Theory of Depression

"How may I help you?" is a question I have asked a great many clients who have come to me for psychological services. More times than I can remember the answer has been, "I'm depressed."

Over the years it became clear to me that depression was an enormous problem because practically everyone I had ever counseled, or even met socially, had gone through literally dozens of depressive episodes, most of them mild, but occasionally some of them rather deep. When I compare the frequency of depression with other common emotional disturbances, I must conclude that fear is about as frequent as depression but that anger is the only psychological condition more frequent. I will deal with anger just a bit in this book because some rather good material has been published on the subject lately. But depression is still somewhat of a no-man's-land, a condition that has been written about at some length, to be sure, but not in a way that offers the average reader much help. Small wonder some of the authors who posed as authorities on the subject have committed suicide!

I would be very much surprised if I killed myself, because I know something about psychological disturbances (depression in particular) which those earlier writers did not know. That is why I am writing this book: to pass on to others some of the newest thinking about neurosis and to offer them a new theory of depression which I have formulated and tested in well over a hundred cases.

Best of all, I find that applying this theory of depression to my own moods can get me over episodes that would ordinarily have put me in a tailspin. But before I practiced this new thinking I had as many problems with the blues as you have. Being rejected used to make me feel inferior and guilty and I would have to stay by myself for hours or days before I came out of it. If I did a job poorly or earned poor grades, that really bothered me and I would have to fight my way out. But again it would take hours or days. And when I was treated unfairly I could feel as sorry for myself as the next fellow.

Well, thank God that was long ago. I have had lots of things happen to me and not all of them have been apple pie. I admit I have been lucky enough to be happily married, to have three lovely girls, and to have parents in good health. Nor have I been unemployed since leaving graduate school. So perhaps I have not had the same cause to be depressed seriously that others can point to. I am sure I would have reacted badly to a misfortune in any of those departments of my life. In fact, any of the usual misfortunes would still jolt me today, but I am also sure I would handle them so much better now than I could have before I learned about depression and how to handle it. As a result, I have not been depressed for so many years I cannot honestly count them. I can roll with the punches (provided they are not overwhelming) and I have taught hundreds of others to do the same. And this is the important point, when you get right down to it. It is not the catastrophic events that one must learn to handle as much as it is the little things that happen almost every day. If we can take daily disappointments, failures, or rejections on the chin, we have practically gotten on top of the depression problem.

It was once thought that depression was something your parents passed down to you, like your brown hair and blue eyes. That's why so little was done with this condition for so long. People gave up hope trying to change something supposedly given them by heredity. But, as opinion began to change, doctors tried medicine and electric shock, and both worked up to a point, especially with the more severe depressions. Milder depression, however, the sort you would talk over with your husband, wife, or best friend, never received much professional attention and so failed to be studied and explained. True, Freud saw the obvious connection between guilt and depression, but he had to louse it up by insisting that the guilt was caused when a child gets sexy ideas over his parents. Some of his other ideas made some sense, but again they weren't much help to the fellow on the street who just got fired from his job.

It may well be that we are born with a tendency toward depressions: some of us have more, some less, than others. This fact, however, can hardly account for the whole cause for feeling blue. If it did, there would be little that anyone could do about the condition. Instead, let us not forget that we are able to *teach* people how to get over depression, so it would only seem reasonable that someone else *taught* them to be depressed in the first place. That's right! When you get upset in any way at all, you are doing what comes fairly naturally, because you inherited an imperfect head and you were taught and well trained to be neurotic by a whole pack of people who also inherited imperfect heads. Practically everywhere you look, in the magazines, in the movies, or on television, and no matter to whom you listen, whether it be your parents, teachers, or friends, you are being trained to be neurotic by these forces and don't know it. They have taught you to be a first-class depressive and now it is up to you to undo the damage they unwittingly did to you.

That is where psychotherapy and this book come in. You must now learn new ways to think to create new attitudes about people and events. How can you do it? By considering depression as a subject to study just as you would geometry, history, or art. Consider counseling to be a course in healthy living, given by a teacher who assigns you reading, asks you to come to a classroom-office once a week or less, and conducts his class for one pupil usually but sometimes a group of students.

What I am really getting at is that you don't need to feel that there is something different or weird about yourself because you have the blues. You are the way you are mainly because you were trained to be that way in exactly the same way you learned to speak the language of your parents. What you learned was mostly junk, but you learned it well. If you can do that, then it should not be too hard to learn some sensible ideas for a change. You have proved that you are able to grasp neurotic ideas. What is to prevent you from grasping healthy ideas? It won't be as easy as it sounds, but it can be done. Millions have done it, some in remarkably short time. The only reason more can't do it is that they don't know how to do it. I intend to show you or at least start you on the way toward successful counseling.

Yes, a book can actually get some of you over your depressive habits. It isn't as important *how* an idea is communicated as it is *what* idea is communicated. Reading is one good way, but listening to lectures is another, taking school courses is another, and tape recordings are another. A number of my clients are encouraged to bring cassette recorders to their therapy sessions so that they can listen to the tapes during the following week and review all the information I gave them during the session. Many have gained a great deal from this approach because they could study the points being made and they had lots of time to think through the new thinking offered them. That's not treatment, that's reeducation! And that is what you need, to learn what you are doing wrong, to learn which of your thinking habits are hurting you and which habits you should replace them with.

I do not want to appear grandiose and suggest that any kind of depression can be eliminated by reading a book. That would be totally unrealistic because depression can exist in any degree of severity. One can feel mildly blue because an expected phone call does not come, and then again, one can feel so guilty over an auto accident that hospitalization and shock therapy are needed. This book will help those with the milder problems the most. But it can help the more depressed also. Even if a severe problem is made less severe instead of being totally conquered, wouldn't it be worth the effort to learn how we depress ourselves and just how to go about reducing depression?

There are some depressions that are caused by physical factors, not by psychological ones. The former should be dealt with by your family physician, your psychiatrist, or perhaps even by a change in diet. Some depressions, especially when you seem to get depressed for no apparent reason, may be the result of a condition called hypoglycemia. This means that the blood has very little glucose, the food required by every cell in the body. Hypoglycemics feel restless, dizzy, irritable, or depressed, or all of these. Some authorities think that persons who have certain forms of mental retardation and schizophrenia, and most alcoholics, are all suffering from low blood sugar.

This condition can be detected by, among other procedures, having seven samples of blood taken over a five-hour period to see how rapidly a previously swallowed sweet drink is absorbed into the blood. If it is absorbed quickly, hypoglycemia is suspected. A change in diet from carbohydrates to proteins is usually advised. Some clients with whom I was counseling and getting practically nowhere were finally advised to have a glucose tolerance test and in most cases it was discovered that they had this condition. When they changed their diets to include meat, dairy products, nuts, and fish, and left out the starches, such as potatoes, spaghetti, rice, cake, pastry, and candy, and gave up coffee, beer, and wine, their nervousness practically ceased, their depressions lifted, and they appeared to be different people in the most surprising ways.

If you suspect that you fall into the category of the hypoglycemic, see your physician and have this question answered before you spend a lot of time and money on psychotherapy. If, however, you can usually point to something in your life that you believe started the depression, then you probably have a case of psychological depression and should read on.

Three Causes of Depression

1. Self-blame

If you are constantly cutting yourself down, hating yourself, thinking that you are the worst human being alive and that you should be horsewhipped every Tuesday and Thursday afternoon, you will get depressed just as sure as there are mental hospitals in the United States. It makes practically no difference what you blame yourself for, just as long as you give yourself a good tongue-lashing over it. It may have resulted because you did not get a promotion, or because you did not win the annual hog-calling contest, or even because someone failed to say "Hello" to you. Just blame yourself and you have a depression coming on. And if you blame yourself mightily, you will become quite disturbed, probably feel like crying, become silent and moody, and you may even want to jump off the Brooklyn Bridge.

If you blame yourself just a little bit, you will only feel uncomfortable and certainly moody. This condition will not be a serious one, but it could spoil a date for you, ruin a party or a trip, and make those around you wish you weren't along.

2. Self-pity

The second way to get depressed is to feel sorry for yourself. Cry in your beer when you are not treated fairly and you will soon be depressed. Put on a long face just to get the sympathy of others and you're on your way to a depression. Think that the world owes you a living and when you find out just how unfair this world can be you're depressed.

This will come as a real surprise to millions of people, but they had better learn that it is neurotic to insist that others treat us fairly, that our kindnesses be returned with kindness, and that the world has to be a decent place in which to live. If we believe this nonsense, we are sure to become depressed and feel hurt and angry when things don't go the way we think they should go.

You are going to have to learn (if you want to avoid depression, that is) that while you are living on the face of this earth, unfair and unkind behavior in exchange for your loving efforts is the rule rather than the exception, and the sooner you realize that things will always be that way, the healthier a person you will become.

3. *Other-pity*

Just as you can be depressed if you break your own leg, you can become depressed if someone else breaks his. Because there is endless suffering in the world, there is endless opportunity to identify with the troubles of millions of poor souls, to say nothing of those in one's immediate family. There is no denying the fact that their troubles and heartaches are real and sometimes pathetic. But if you pity the child with crutches, if you pity the fellow whose house burned down, if you pity the mother whose son died in the war, you will become just as depressed as if you blamed yourself or pitied yourself. The depression will look the same regardless of which method you are using, and one method can depress you as badly as another. The only thing you can be sure of is that you are in pain of the worst sort.

There you have it, the three reasons why people become emotionally depressed. In the following pages you will learn why you blame yourself and think you are right to do so, why you pity yourself and feel correct and justified in doing so, and why you pity others and feel squeamish about doing otherwise. Furthermore, you will also learn why you are wrong, foolish, and totally mistaken to hate yourself under *any* conditions, why pitying yourself only makes you your own worst enemy, and why pitying others undermines their self-confidence. You will learn how you justify these actions and how you will have to change your beliefs to avoid future depressions.

So read on, depressives of the world. You have nothing to lose but your tears!

2

Bad Me!

Wʜᴇɴ I ᴛᴇʟʟ ᴍʏ ᴄʟɪᴇɴᴛs ᴛʜᴀᴛ ᴛʜᴇʏ ᴡᴏᴜʟᴅ ʙᴇ ᴍᴜᴄʜ better off never to feel guilt, they look at me as though I had lost my senses. "How is it possible never to feel guilt when it is impossible to behave perfectly?" they ask. The answer is really quite simple: admit that you *are* guilty when you have done something you think was wrong, immoral, or needlessly painful to others. Do that and nothing more. I guarantee that you will be so undisturbed over your objectionable behavior that you will begin to look at your actions in a calm and objective way, and you will even think it through so that you can probably avoid doing it again in the future.

What most people do, however, is admit that they may have behaved badly, that is, they see the fact that they *are* guilty of wrong behavior and then they *feel* guilty over that behavior. It is that second step which causes the trouble. It is the step which convinces them that they are terrible, evil, and worthless people because they behaved badly.

And what does it mean to feel guilt? It means that you have *labeled* yourself by your behavior. Your thinking usually goes something like this: "I am guilty of being rude to that waiter. That means I am bad." "I am guilty of belittling my wife. I am worthless."

Can you see what you have been doing? You have been *judging yourself by your behavior*. If you behave well, you think you're great. If you behave badly, you think you're a rat. But should you? Must we rate ourselves? Must we pin a star on our chests for being kind to an old lady crossing the street and must we hate ourselves if we push an old lady into the street?

You're immediately going to tell me that we *should* feel guilty for doing something so rotten. You're going to insist that there has to be something terribly wrong with anyone who would hurt an old lady, chew out an innocent waiter, or pick needless fights with his wife. And you're going to decide that what is so rotten about that person is his worthlessness, wickedness, evilness, and just plain badness. Not so. There is always a good reason why you may have behaved badly, a reason so good, in fact, that you have every right in the world to forgive yourself.

Three Reasons for Never Blaming Yourself

1. Stupidity

By stupidity I mean not having the intelligence to do as well as you'd like to do. If a person is mentally retarded, we can hardly expect him to behave in a faultless way. And even if he were not intellectually retarded, he could still be so limited in his intelligence in specialized ways that we could easily forgive him for doing badly. Let's take the example of the retarded child first.

Johnny has an I.Q. of about 60. He is about eight years old and loves to pick up things and finger them. One day he comes into your home, finds a book of

28

matches and plays with them. Accidentally he sets the room on fire and someone gets hurt. What he has done is a most unfortunate thing, but would we say *he* is a bad and evil child? I hope not. It was, after all, not his wickedness that drove him to play with the matches, it was a child's curiosity. His low intelligence prevented him from sensing the danger he was in. Therefore, it was only natural that he would start a fire and perhaps even hurt someone. Even if he had burned down the whole apartment building and killed everyone in it, the facts would remain unchanged. Johnny would *be* guilty of a very bad act but would be foolish to *feel* guilty over it since he was behaving in the only way retarded children can act around matches: unintelligently. It would also be foolish for the adults concerned about Johnny to scold him, to call him bad names, and to try to make him depressed. In short, we could separate the child's behavior from himself. We could judge the act without also judging the child. His actions were bad, he was not.

Suppose now we take a more likely example, this time a young girl, your daughter, and we want her to play the piano. It seems, however, that she has very little talent for this instrument—or for music, for that matter. So she inevitably does poorly at the instrument, learns slowly, and has no feel for the music. In a word, she is unintelligent where music is concerned. She cannot carry a melody, and the only interest she ever shows in music is for the latest tunes all her friends seem to know. It is as though, in this one area of her life, she is retarded and incapable of ever doing well. Johnny is retarded in intellectual matters, while your daughter is retarded in musical matters. Neither has the mental equipment ever to master the skill in which each is deficient.

Would you think that your daughter was an evil and

bad girl merely because she played the piano badly? I would certainly hope not. In fact, most parents see the handwriting on the wall and usually let up on the girl and just chalk up as a lost cause their attempt to get a concert pianist. The temptation to rate the girl by her inferior piano-playing usually doesn't occur to us, because nothing really bad has happened. Should that matter, though? Isn't the reason why your daughter does badly similar to the reason why Johnny does badly? Then if you want to be consistent, you will have to separate the behavior of each child from the child and judge that behavior as unacceptable or dangerous without also judging the child as being worthless.

2. Ignorance

Johnny and your daughter did not have the mental equipment ever to learn certain skills. Suppose a person does something really bad and is not retarded. Should we then conclude that that person is worthless, bad, and evil?

You are a young father. Your wife took the evening off and left you to care for your new baby. The child cries and you find that his diapers need changing. One of the big safety pins that keeps the diaper snug gets jammed, so you carelessly push too forcefully to open it and stick the baby real hard.

Again it makes sense to say that you *are* guilty of hurting the baby, but surely you would agree that you don't need to *feel* guilty. You wouldn't, of course, feel glad over the mistake. That would be very neurotic of you, to say the least.

Feeling guilty, however, would mean that you think you *should not* have stuck the baby, and that is foolish. You are, after all, a clumsy, inexperienced father who

30

loves his child and wants to make him comfortable. To suppose, however, that you can perform a delicate act like changing a diaper and can do so perfectly with your limited experience does not make sense. Under the circumstances it would be rather surprising if you did not hurt the child from time to time and until you gained more skill. Your problem is not that you are a dirty dog for hurting your boy, your problem is that you are ignorant of how to perform that job smoothly. More practice will fix the matter nicely.

Ignorance means that you have not yet learned a skill, whereas stupidity means that you can never learn it no matter how much practice you get. Even a genius can be ignorant and not do a great many things well until he has had the opportunity to learn them.

Mothers often have a big problem with feeling guilty over the poor job they have done in raising their children. Perhaps the children have taken to drugs, become pregnant, or dropped out of school. When such instances are studied carefully it is easy to find numerous examples of poor child-rearing practices. In fact, I often tell these mothers that I agree with them, that they are lousy mothers and have done a bad job, but I immediately stress the fact that they have no legitimate right to hate themselves for their many blunders. Whatever they did in the way of raising their children they did with the best of intentions and love. They may have loved too much, or been too eager to protect their children from making serious mistakes and nagged them in the hope that the children would straighten up. When this technique didn't work they probably became more controlling, more scolding and blaming, and unwittingly more inefficient as mothers.

Their problem was not that they are worthless people,

just poor mothers. And why shouldn't they be? Many of them had emotional problems of their own. Most, however, did not have the right information on how to handle many of the problems the children were sure to give them. If they were ignorant on how to deal with a rebellious youngster, should they scold themselves and *feel* guilty because they *are* guilty? That attitude may have contributed to the problem initially.

I take a very different attitude about such mistakes. I point out to these women that most of them have never had a course in psychology. Many of them have not read the best books on the subject of child-rearing. Others did not realize that one or two sessions with a psychotherapist could have put them on the right track and given them techniques to use that might have worked much better than their own. Since they did not know any of this, I urge them not to be too hard on themselves or feel guilty over their faulty rearing of their children, because they could not do what they were not taught. Most of them were merely following the faulty techniques practiced on them by their own well-meaning parents. And why shouldn't they? They speak the language of their parents. They follow their customs, eat similar food, play the same card games, and so on. All these practices were learned from their parents, so why shouldn't the child-rearing methods they saw all their lives being practiced on them also be imitated?

Again, it is their ignorance, their lack of knowledge of better methods, which created their problems with the children, not some rotten quality within them that they should blame themselves for.

Now let's look at a really serious case. Suppose a high school student is learning to drive. He comes to a road crossing at lunchtime just as a group of children are crossing. Instead of stepping on the brake pedal, he accidentally steps on the gas, goes through the intersection, and kills several of the children.

It goes without saying that the parents of these children would be very much disturbed over this tragedy and would want to lynch the boy. His parents might also be furious with him and beat him or scold him to within an inch of his life. And worst of all, the boy himself would be quite inclined to blame himself so severely that he would almost certainly depress himself. He *was* the guilty party who killed the children. Shouldn't he *feel* guilty too?

No! He should not feel guilty, because he has an excellent reason for having the accident: he is inexperienced, untrained, and still very awkward behind the wheel of a car. If he had had more practice, he would most certainly not have made such a blunder. Again, he is guilty because he was ignorant, not bad.

You may have the feeling in your heart that something is wrong, even dangerous with this way of thinking. If we don't blame people for their serious mistakes, if we don't want them to feel guilty over someone's death, then what is to stop people from doing so all the time and not even minding it either?

You have forgotten that stupid and ignorant people did not want to behave badly in the first place, or that they did not realize that their behavior was wrong even while engaged in it (as with the retarded population). In any event, you are of course quite correct that something must be done about retarded boys who could walk into your house and accidentally set it on fire. And we must certainly do something about the young driver so that he does not get so confused when coming to a cross-walk that he cannot tell which pedal is the brake and which is the accelerator.

In the first case we will try to be more careful about leaving our doors unattended so that the neighborhood children cannot wander in anytime they take a notion to explore. We can also see to it that we keep matches out of the reach of children, and do the same with guns, knives, and other dangerous objects.

For the youths taking driving lessons, we could perhaps give them more exercises for reacting quickly to the brake, and do this in the safety of the school grounds, on an isolated road, or in a cornfield, before letting them drive city streets. That is what we should do about preventing these kinds of accidents. Screaming at the person after the damage is done does pitifully little good and may do a great deal of harm. We confuse him with so much guilt feeling that he often does not stop to think about how the accident happened in the first place and what he should do to avoid it again in the future.

3. Disturbance

By now the thought will have occurred to you that there is one class of behaviors that are not forgivable: those which are committed deliberately with full knowledge of what the consequences will be. Take the case of a bright fellow in college who has an I.Q. of about 130 but who is goofing off so badly that he is ready to be expelled from school. He knows that he is in danger of being thrown out. He knows that doing his homework and giving up girls and booze would permit him to pass his course easily. So you are inclined to insist that he should feel guilty because he is intelligent and knows

34

what is happening to his career. Still he stupidly heads straight for disaster.

Apparently we cannot excuse his behavior on the grounds that he is stupid (retarded) or ignorant. We can, however, excuse it on the grounds that he would have to be disturbed. How else are we going to comprehend such foolish behavior? In other words, such a person is not evil or worthless because he is wasting his parents' money and disappointing them sorely. Such a person is neurotic, vengeful, or afraid. Such a person has emotional hang-ups which make him act as though he were an idiot. And if you had his emotional blocks, you would probably act the same way.

I have known a number of promising students who did exactly what the fellow in the example did. When these problems were analyzed they always boiled down to the fellow's being so afraid that he would not live up to the godlike expectations of his parents that he just couldn't stand to face the defeat he knew he would experience if he really tried. When you have been told all your life that you are great and smart, and are sure to be a success by becoming the president of a New York bank, you have a heavy burden to live up to. Rather than let your folks know that you might just be an ordinary guy, you let yourself fail because you can always blame the failure on your not trying, rather than on a limited ability which they always insisted you did not have. Then you can even feel less guilt by saying you failed school because you played around, rather than because you weren't a genius after all.

You must admit that that is an emotional problem: a fear of disappointing your parents, a fear of having to tell them that they had you wrong all along. Now suppose it isn't fear at all. Then it might be spite, another

35

serious emotional problem. In this case your parents forced you into medicine, but you really hate it. By goofing off you get back at them for not letting you become an artist, even if it hurts you also. Your grades are suffering all across the board, grades you will need if you are ever to go into art school, and they are being fouled up along with those you would need for the medical courses. You are also developing some powerfully bad habits that you will someday have to overcome if and when you can get your parents to change their minds. You know all this, but you can't do a thing about it. You are neurotic, and all the reasoning in the world will not change your behavior for the time being. Your goal in life is either to avoid looking inadequate, since you think that you are worthless unless you are an "A" student, or to be so angry with your parents that nothing else matters.

Never Blame Yourself for Anything, Anytime, Anywhere

When you *feel* guilty because you *are* guilty over some misdeed, you are blaming yourself. That is one of the most unhealthy acts you can perform. It is one I want to teach you never to commit and in the following pages I hope to show you why you are neurotic if you blame yourself, what self-blame leads to, and how to fight it. First, let me explain for a moment exactly what I mean by blame.

Blame involves a double attack: one against your actions, the other against yourself as a person. If you spill ink on the furniture, you are only sensible to call yourself clumsy. You are not sensible, however, to attack yourself and call yourself all sorts of ugly names because you may be clumsy. You may be careless. You may be uncoordinated. You may even do it because you are spiteful. But you are not a bum because of any of these reasons. If you think you are, then you have already blamed yourself.

I know of a man who accidentally killed a pedestrian in a car accident. Naturally he strongly disapproved of his careless driving, but he decided that because he had been the unwitting cause of another man's death he was a worthless louse who should never forgive himself. That is blame. He blamed himself for years. He was depressed on and off, to a greater or lesser degree, for about ten years of his life before he learned that his depression and self-blame were quite neurotic.

Self-blame is like giving yourself a report card. In school it is fairly accurate to say that you are an "A" student in geography or history, a "B" student in English, etc. That doesn't make *you* an "A" or a "B" person, though. You must separate the subject from yourself as a human being. If you do not do this, you will believe that you are fine when you receive "A's" and worthless when you receive "F's." This is precisely what is often done. And the same applies to nonschool subjects. It applies to everyday behavior. A woman who goes against her religious teachings and has an abortion performed on herself may very likely have performed an immoral act in her eyes, but she also becomes an *immoral human being* in her own eyes. She rates her*self* by her actions. That means that the only times she will be a worthwhile person is when she behaves perfectly and above fault. It is obvious that people who follow this philosophy are doomed to be depressed a good deal of the time, for how often can any of us ever behave in a faultless manner?

At this point in counseling, my clients usually raise this question: "How can I separate my behavior from

37

myself? My actions are me." In the following chapter I will go into the techniques of overcoming depression and learning to separate one's behavior from oneself. For the present I want first to convince you of the utter danger of self-blame by showing all the unfortunate consequences that result from it.

Blame Is a Violent Act Against You

Stop for a moment and think what you do to yourself when you blame yourself. First you think of yourself as unworthy of belonging to the human race. You see yourself as a species apart from all others. You smear yourself with verbal filth so that you stink to yourself even if others cannot smell you. You tar and feather yourself with invisible hate and loathing. Sometimes you physically punish yourself with burning cigarettes or you cut yourself with razor blades. And always you treat yourself as though others should spit on you and avoid you like the plague. Now that is violence, wouldn't you agree?

Suppose now that someone else were to do all these acts to you. Wouldn't you think he was the meanest and cruelest human being you had ever met? Wouldn't you wonder if he was a nut? And wouldn't you fight for your very life not to be treated in such a shameful way? Of course you would. You would have to be crazy not to. But do you stop this violence when it is *you* who is doing it? Not on your life. You relish it. You think you have it coming to you. It even feels good to you because you believe that through all of this self-torture you are cleansing yourself of all your sins.

If it is so good to suffer when *you* do it, why is it wrong if someone else does it? In fact, if you want to be sensible and realistic about it, all you self-blamers should go to jail and really get a dose of punishment, or volunteer for suicide squads, or work in leper colonies. Strange as it seems, this is precisely what some consistent self-blamers actually do. They expose themselves to danger, bankruptcy, failure, all in the belief that they have it coming to them because they stink. Most self-blamers, however, do not go this far. They punish themselves in private, curse their existence to themselves while trying to hide their self-hatred from others, and do not see the point at all that they are being monstrously unfair to themselves.

Blame Is Always Dangerous

Not only is blame wrong and evil when directed at you, by yourself, it is wrong and dangerous when directed at others. In the latter case it generates hatred, anger, and violence. If you will remember what I just finished pointing out about blame against oneself, you will easily see why blame against others does the same. When others behave badly you are naturally inclined to rate them as bad also. They become the same as their deeds. Good deeds, and you think you are dealing with good humans. Bad deeds, and you deal with bad people. Rubbish! Good deeds do not make good people. Good deeds make good carpenters (or whatever), but who says that good carpenters are good humans? Bad deeds make bad parents (or whatever), but who is to say that bad parents are bad and worthless humans? Again we confuse the person with his actions.

Practically all the violence, war, torture, and murder in the world can be traced to this awful belief that (a) there are bad people in the world and (b) bad people should be severely blamed and punished for their evil acts. Certainly they should be locked up for our safety, but to kill or punish them is doing no more than they did to come to our attention.

Take the murderer, for example. He is frustrated for some reason and in his immaturity and impulsiveness decides that someone is in his way. That person is regarded by the murderer as a wicked person: he has blamed the other fellow for something he did. The philosophy of blame tells him that the other fellow is wicked and should be bumped off. We as a society do not tolerate people going around judging people by their actions and then punishing them for it. So we take this murderer and sentence him to the electric chair. Wow! Can you see what society has done? It has blamed the murderer in precisely the same way that the murderer blamed his victim and now it is committing the same unacceptable act on the murderer that the murderer committed on his victim. It was wrong when John Dillinger killed someone, but it is all right when we killed Dillinger!

Let's not go to extremes. Most of us don't even know a murderer, so a look at an everyday occurrence would help explain the dangers of blame a great deal better. Your husband just bought a car and didn't consult you about it. You didn't even want another car, but you are willing to overlook that. However, the rat didn't even give you a chance to select the model or color! And after all you have done for him! You have been more than fair with him. You don't spend a cent without first consulting with him. Now you decide that this is terribly unfair (and you are absolutely correct), so you decide to hit him with everything about him that has ever bothered you. When you are done warming up with a good tongue-lashing, you throw something at him, and for the finale you try to make him feel utterly lousy by going to your bedroom and bawling. If you have a bathroom with a lock on it, that is even better.

This is not a fairy tale. It is the unvarnished truth as it takes place across our fair land in practically every household by husbands and wives every so often. In some households it is as daily a ritual as washing dishes (if there are any left to wash).

The wife in the above example has blamed her husband for being thoughtless. In effect she says to herself: "He *behaved* wrongly. *He is* bad." And 99 percent of the world would agree with her. No, make it 99.999 percent of the world. I protest. Fifty million Frenchmen *can* be wrong. How is she wrong? For one thing, her husband is a human being, made imperfectly just as she was. That means he must have some faults. If she doesn't want thoughtlessness as one of his big faults, then what would she be satisfied with? Would she be happier if he were a rapist? or a child molester? or an embezzler? No? Then perhaps she ought to accept him with this fault and go about calmly trying to break him of this habit instead of giving him reason to hate her so much he just might go out and buy an elephant without consulting her.

This kind of blame is dangerous because it drives people away, it breaks up marriages, it helps create guilt and depression in the victim, and it plays hell with your blood pressure and ulcers. That is right, you probably never thought of just how your righteous anger is cooking your goose too. One cannot be furious at another without paying a price. I have known some people who were told by their doctors that they had bad hearts and should not get upset for any reason. Yet these same people go on, day after day, getting sore about a million

41

things and *they* have to pay the price for it. Someone once said that anger was the price *you* paid for another person's mistakes. How do you like that?

Self-blamers Are Conceited

When you think back over how low you have been at times when you felt very guilty you can probably remember only how inferior you felt, how untouchable you must have seemed to others, and how totally unworthy you had become. Depressed persons can usually be described as humble, lacking self-confidence, and having a very low opinion of themselves. To suggest that these self-loathers are fundamentally conceited sounds preposterous. Yet, such is clearly the case.

An adolescent girl whom I recently counseled for depression told me that she had become pregnant and felt like killing herself. She went on to say that she felt dirty and ashamed. For all the world her behavior could be described as anything but conceit. That is why it almost knocked her out of the chair when I suggested that she was one of the most conceited persons I had ever met.

"Me? Conceited?" she asked in amazement.

"Yes, you. You think you're so unbelievably good that you shouldn't make mistakes or blunder in any way at all."

"But that's true. I shouldn't have become pregnant. I knew better, but I let it happen anyway."

"What if one of your girl friends had gotten pregnant? Would you blame her? Would you want to kill her? Would you refuse to speak to her? Would you shun her company just as you think others should shun you? Like hell you would. Unless you're very different from most people, you'd go up to your girl friend, put your arm around her, and give her all the support and love you could show. And you'd mean it too."

"Yes," she said, "I'm sure I would. But isn't that different?"

"I suppose it is," I answered. "People like her are expected to get knocked up. But superhuman persons like yourself, well, that's different. *You* aren't supposed to foul up. *You* can't be impulsive and overly romantic. That's what one expects from the common herd, like your girl friend. But *you*, ah, that's different. I suppose you must belong to a different species of mankind."

With more debate she began to see my reasoning. It gradually dawned on her that she was being utterly grandiose when she could not forgive herself for a careless act, whereas she would not hesitate to do the same for her friend.

This is an underlying trait of all self-blamers. They cannot stand the ugly fact that they are just human, faulty, mistake makers, and no amount of work will ever change that trait completely. Still they go on endlessly, neurotically demanding that their behavior has to be better than others' and that unless they stop their wrongdoings immediately, they deserve the worst kind of treatment. It is high time we fully appreciated what it means to be human.

Suppose you were God and you decided to populate your planets with perfect creatures. You could make them all wise, with supercolossal intelligence, amazingly quick reflexes, and completely without periods of youth or old age. After all, even God cannot make a perfect baby, because by definition a baby is an undeveloped and ignorant creature. And God would want to eliminate the aged, for how else could he have a world full of error-free people if he allowed them to grow old and

43

senile and thereby lose the alertness that made these people so perfect? He would, therefore, have to create people who are born with young bodies and middle-aged minds, and that is the way they would be forever, or until they died (assuming that God wanted them to live for only a specified period). There would be no aging process as we know it, for that would surely introduce faulty behavior. Therefore, in a universe of perfect beings it would have to be "Here today, gone tomorrow."

On the other hand, if you were God, you could decide to make the creatures who will inherit your universe imperfect. But if you did that, your expectations of these poor mortals ought certainly to be quite different from the expectations of a planet full of perfect beings. From mortals we should expect a long period of learning, as long as sixteen or eighteen years before these creatures could even consider being on their own. And as these mortals got older we would expect them to lose their quickness, their intellectual sharpness, and to deteriorate slowly in all respects. But even during their best years we would expect these normal human beings to do all manner of dumb and stupid things. In other words, we would expect some of these people to commit murder, suicide, theft, and all manner of atrocities. Mothers from this group will beat their babies to death. Fathers from this group will declare wars for their sons to die in. These people will hate very easily as well as love very easily. Though they will be capable of remarkable achievements, such as skyscrapers, conquest of diseases, and outer space exploration, these same people have to mess up their great work by polluting their air, saving so many people that their planet threatens to become overpopulated, and build so many atomic bombs that their entire world could be blown apart.

Sounds weird? Why should it be? All of this sounds perfectly reasonable to me because I really do accept the fact that man is man, that man is imperfect, and that he cannot help being a plain sap a great deal of the time. So I expect the worst from imperfect people, while I try to help them fight these very weaknesses and to make the most of the intelligence which is not used up in being stupid.

Despite the sense this analysis makes, there are millions of people who will still go on saying that man should not become violent, that one's children should not die, and that accidents should not happen. How stupid can we be?

How much better it would be to say: "It would be *better* if we were not so violent. How much *nicer* existence would be if our loved ones did not die on us. And wouldn't it be *wonderful* if we did not have accidents?" These statements make sense because they express wishes and preferences, not demands or necessities. Demanding something merely because you want something is certain to lead to disturbance if you do not get your way. Rather than get upset by getting angry at your wife, stop demanding perfect behavior from yourself in the ridiculous, grandiose manner I described above, and accept your actions for the unavoidable conditions they are, and you are sure to be more self-loving as well as other-loving. Give up your conceit. I have news for you: God chose to make people according to the second plan I outlined, not the first.

Self-blamers Are Cowards

Guilt is a fantastically successful method of keeping people from committing certain acts. Murder is less frequent than it is, not only because one gets a stiff jail sentence or death penalty for it but because one's sense of conscience would be so severe that we dread living with such a possibility. People all over the world have behaved in a law-abiding way because their sense of guilt would hurt them too much to do otherwise. There is no denying the efficiency of making our guilty consciences the guardians over our conduct.

Unfortunately the price we pay for using guilt in this manner is enormous, for not only does it prevent us from behaving badly, it very frequently prevents us from behaving courageously and sensibly. When Shakespeare pointed out that conscience makes cowards of us all, he was expressing this very idea. I would like to show you how a guilty conscience can make such a weakling out of you that you end up allowing others to best you, to take the most unkind advantage of you, and in general to make you deny your own interests to the point where you wonder if you have a mind of your own, or if your life belongs to you.

Bill was a particularly good example of what happens to a person who feels guilty. Once during his marriage he had an affair, but his wife never found out about it. Afraid she would reject him, Bill kept the secret to himself for over ten years. During this time he felt that he had no right to assert himself against his wife's unreasonable behavior, and she, sensing that he would never fight for his own rights, tended to take ever greater advantage of him. It got so bad between them that he hated her for her unreasonableness, he hated himself for being a coward and not kicking her in the pants, and she hated him because he never showed any gumption and let her figuratively wipe her feet on him.

During a session with him alone I learned about his

affair and how he justified his weakness and fear. He could see quite easily that he had acted very cowardly over the years, but he could not understand me at all when I insisted that he had no need to feel guilty over the affair, and that the sooner he confessed to his wife, the sooner she could not hold that invisible guilt over his head.

Our discussions soon revealed how good he felt with a woman who would not point out his shortcomings constantly, and that it was for this reassurance of his own esteem that he started and continued the affair. I insisted, however, that he did this because of low self-esteem, a psychological problem, not some wickedness, some rottenness that he had to live with for the rest of his life. If he could learn to accept himself and stop being a self-blamer, even his wife could not throw him for a loop. So what point would there be in having an affair that supposedly built his ego but did so at the cost of making him chickenhearted?

When Bill reached the point where he could honestly see that he had a right to act like a jerk, he found it easy to confess his indiscretions to his wife, and, as predicted, their relationship changed greatly after she got over the initial shock.

"When I realize all the crap I've taken all these years," Bill later said, "I could kick myself all over town. Just because I did one thing for which I was not proud, I let that woman have her way, let her say things to me, make demands of the nuttiest sort, and I just felt I had to take it. Well, that's over and I'm glad, I can tell you. Why, all the while I thought I was scum, it never occurred to me to ask what the hell she was doing that was all that great. If I had treated her the way she treated me, what with all her selfishness, I would have had plenty to blame myself for. But do you think for one moment she gave herself a bad time over taking advantage of me like I did by being unfaithful to her? Brother, when that hit me between the eyes I stopped being her patsy or anybody's patsy. Sure I will goof up again, but I'll be damned if I'll get on that self-blame merry-go-round again."

A bonus came along with Bill's new-found assertiveness: his wife gained new respect for him. As she put it: "Of course I think more of Bill now. Why, to compare his strength now with the weak and scared kid I was married to before makes me realize that maybe all along I was hoping to make him so sick of my picking on him that he would finally get some guts and act like a man. When you helped him overcome his sense of guilt because of that other woman, he changed inside of a week."

One of the most interesting and unusual consequences of a guilty conscience was observed in a teen-age girl who was not only depressed but heard voices telling her to kill her mother or to kill herself. The two of them battled a good deal, and there were the usual scenes and ugly words hurled back and forth when things got very nasty. Though the mother meant well and wanted only to correct her daughter she failed to realize how hostile and hateful the girl was becoming at being told how to run her life all day. It took a few years of this sort of warfare before the hatred got so intense that the girl did not even want to recognize it. That is when she developed the auditory hallucinations.

Sometimes she could ignore the voices, but often they bothered her during a normal conversation, such as when talking to a friend or making a purchase. This really unnerved her because she couldn't carry on two conversations at once and she couldn't let on to the person she was listening to that she should be excused a moment because she had something to say to the thin air.

The first time I learned about this symptom was during a group therapy session. I asked the other group members to suggest what the girl might do to stop the voices. Their thoughts ran along the following line: find an excuse to leave the scene; talk up more loudly to drown out the murderous suggestions; begin laughing to convince herself the whole thing was ridiculous; and finally, say nothing until the voices ceased. I explained why none of these solutions would probably work and then told them what I thought would do the trick. A female member of the group almost fainted when I suggested, "We've got to convince her not to feel guilty for wanting to kill her mother."

Let me explain my thinking this way: the more you worry about a thing happening, the more likely it is to happen. This young lady was always very conscious and aware of these threatening voices and she was quite alarmed by them as well. They never would have gotten out of control had she not made an earthshaking event out of having the feelings of murder in the first place. Had she taken them calmly, she could have laughed them off easily enough. To this end I advised her to consider her anger as being fairly normal, to realize that she had had these feelings a number of times—probably hundreds—and still had never acted upon them, and to forgive her mother for frustrating her so since her mother too was only human and trying her best to help her daughter. Each time the voices appeared she was to react as calmly as possible, do nothing about suppressing them, feel no guilt, and in time they would certainly diminish in importance.

Inside of one month the voices had gone almost completely. If they returned sporadically, she analyzed her angry feelings and talked herself out of them. And because no one in the group thought she was an awful human being for hating her mother, she lost her sense of panic over them. It was only then that she confronted her mother in a healthy way and did not allow herself to be dominated. This action prevented the numerous frustrations that normally set her off.

The last example of guilt making cowards of us is that of John. He was an alcoholic who frequently got drunk because his father wanted someone to drink with and to make the rounds of the bars with. John was now in AA and trying his best to stay dry, but every once in a while he would come to me depressed because he would refuse to drink with dear old dad, and on one recent occasion he refused to let his dad take his three children with him on his tour of the bars. At such times, the father would appeal directly to John's sense of guilt and review for him all that he had done for John over the years, and how it was John's duty as a son to grant his father these simple favors. John held firm and refused, but it tore him up inside to do so.

I attempted to show John that his dad was being nothing more than an emotional baby by demanding these ridiculous things and that it would hardly kill the old boy if he weren't satisfied. Then I showed John how he could very easily deny his dad a great number of favors without feeling guilty if he could decide in his own mind that the issues were important.

"John, if your dad told you he had a strong hankering to burn your house down just so he could have some excitement, you surely wouldn't let him go ahead and do it, would you?"

"Of course not."

"Or suppose your dad wanted to use your living room

for a toilet, would you let him?"

"Of course not."

"But, John, suppose he told you how a son is supposed to please his dad, how you owe him for years of devotion, how he thinks you are ungrateful, inconsiderate, and so on because you won't let him burn down your house or use your rug as a place to relieve himself. Would any of that make any difference?"

"I know what you're getting at, doc, but that's different."

"Different? What's so different about those examples and what the old boy has actually done to you already? He's helped make you an alcoholic and practically ruined your marriage, and now he's suggesting he put your girls in danger just so he can have some company. No, John, I can't buy your reasoning. If you can refuse him some items, you can refuse him two more which are immensely important to you."

And he did see the point. Rather than let daddy play with his guilt, John became firm with the old man, accepted the temporary rejection that followed, and did himself and his children a world of good. None of this would have been possible, however, if he had not conquered his guilt.

Feeling Guilty Makes You Behave Worse

People are hung up on the idea that it is moral to feel guilty over misdeeds on the grounds that the pain connected with the guilt will prove to be so unpleasant that the act will surely be avoided in the future. If this is what actually happened, I would be the first to suggest that we develop all the guilt we can and thereby become less and less error prone. Unfortunately this is not the case. In fact, the opposite behavior accomplishes what we have always thought guilt did for us. Namely, don't blame yourself *at all,* but analyze your errors and sins, and then try hard not to do them again. Blaming yourself for your sins convinces you that better behavior is all but impossible and that worse behavior is exactly what a louse like you needs for punishment. Besides, how else can you impress your error on your memory if you don't bleed inside because of it?

Take the case of Lucy. She married, her husband left for the service, she was lonely and had an affair. Although she had moral pangs about this romance, she enjoyed it enough to cancel out any thought of stopping it or of blaming herself severely. But it ended in a half year and she then found herself in the arms of another man just about as soon as the previous fellow had left town. Now she began to hate herself. It was at this point that she decided she must be a whore, a deprived human being who was above help, and who might just as well go forth and lay any fellow who took a liking to her. One night after attending a party, she noticed that one of the males at the party was following her in his car. What did she do? The only consistent thing a "tramp" could do. She stopped her car, walked back to his, and made love. Then she returned to her car and went home. I received a call that evening from a very weepy girl, contemplating suicide, and asking for help.

Only a few sessions were needed to get her to see what she was doing to herself. She changed completely when she realized that self-blame convinced her she was all bad instead of just foolish and unfaithful. I never once agreed with her that her actions were harmless. The way she was jumping around from bed to bed was serious, could give her a disease or make her pregnant, and was terribly unfair to her husband. But I insisted that she did those reckless things because she was so disturbed because of her guilt that she had no choice but to continue her self-punishing tactics. When she realized that, the problem was neatly nipped in the bud.

It will not hurt you much if you blame yourself just a little. It is the severe and constant blame you must watch out for. When you believe that you are unworthy you will see to it that nothing worthy happens to you. The worst enemies we have are ourselves. The boy who is told that he will never amount to anything because he has cheated on a test and that he should be ashamed of all the pain he has caused his mamma—that boy is sure to feel unworthy of his mother's love and he will do whatever it takes to get his mother to detest him. After all, his mother has told him repeatedly that he is not worthy of her love, and can his mother be wrong?

Self-acceptance is the medicine to cure this illness—acceptance of one's weaknesses, one's human faults and habits, while all the time trying hard to overcome these annoying human frailties we all inherit when we are born. Forgiveness for others, but also forgiveness for ourselves is the great lesson the self-blamer must learn.

Religion and Self-blame

To some of you, the points that I have made about never blaming yourself sound wicked and sinful. You might conclude that I advocate all sorts of immoral acts, all sorts of violence, and encourage people to do these things without even feeling bad about them. This is certainly not true. In fact, I maintain that (a) most people who think that they are religious are actually not, (b) most people who think that they are leading a good life as outlined in the Bible are often doing just the opposite, and (*c*) what I have said about never blaming yourself is very Christian and (*d*) is supported by the Bible.

Our religions want us to be happy people, content with ourselves and loving toward others. When we err, we are told by our faiths that it is human to do so. We should forgive ourselves. We should forgive those who trespass against us also. Remember? When you do not blame others for their errors, you are forgiving them for their trespassing, aren't you? And when you truly forgive yourself for your failings and shortcomings, are you not doing as the Bible suggests: loving your neighbor as *yourself*? Notice, this passage from the Bible hits upon both directions at the same time. It tells us to love others, but to love ourselves as well. It could also be translated into: blame not others as you would not blame yourself.

Every religion with which I am familiar makes a point of the human being's recognizing the fact that he is human and that no amount of work or power can make him a god. In other words, all religions accept the fact that man is man, that he is weak, and that he will sin no matter how hard he tries not to sin. He may, of course, be able to reduce his objectionable behavior considerably, but he will never stop it entirely. Man is not perfect, so he must act imperfectly. This means he will steal, cheat, hurt, be selfish, and so on. Only God is perfect, but he made us imperfectly. Therefore, he has the power of forgiveness regardless of what we have done. I know of no church that does not make total forgiveness by God one of its central beliefs.

The point I wish to make is that if God can forgive us our terrible behavior, shouldn't we be equally kind and generous with ourselves? Is it consistent with our religions to say, "I know that God forgives me for my sins,

54

but I can't"? This places our judgment above his. And this is the same point I have made from a psychological viewpoint. We need never blame ourselves for anything, because God made us imperfect. He knew he did it that way the moment he decided to do it, and he doesn't blame us for doing the dumb things that imperfect people are supposed to do.

If you follow these teachings from your religion or your Bible, I have no doubt you will seldom be depressed—at least not from self-blame. This is a perfect example where religion and psychology stand side by side and say almost the same thing. So don't feel guilty if you try to talk yourself out of feeling guilty the next time you misbehave. Remember, you are being unfaithful to your religion if you do feel guilt. It is hoped that you will admit *being* guilty as well as fight *feeling* guilty. You can do this without a sense of having betrayed your religious teachings. Even if your minister insists that you should feel worthless for an act you despise, tell him that he doesn't know his own teachings and hasn't the foggiest notion of what religion is supposed to be all about. Chances are that he gets depressed about as often as you do because he thinks he is beyond redemption and that he is a perfect rat because of some act over which he must hate himself for the rest of his life. When a minister gets emotionally upset, you can assume he hasn't followed his own religious teachings very well. Christianity and Judaism both have many wise statements, which, if interpreted correctly, can make one emotionally healthy for a lifetime. So, when a minister, or anyone for that matter, is not emotionally stable he is not being true to his sacred teachings. I have shown in a book I recently wrote, *Reason in Pastoral Counseling*, that all the essential points of a healthy psychology can be found in the

Bible. The reason so many people are disturbed despite the fact that they are members of churches and have been all their lives is that they read the messages incorrectly and therefore fail to lead truly exemplary lives.

The whole point I am driving at is to warn you depressives that you *are* likely to feel guilty if you do *not* feel guilty over poor behavior. You think that your religious teachings want you to suffer emotionally. You are wrong. Religion should not be a whip, it should be a blanket. If you get depressed, feel guilt, are overcome with fury, or are filled with fear, you are not being psychologically sound, but you are not being true to your faith either.

3

Be Kind to Yourself

ASSUMING THAT YOU AGREE WITH ME SO FAR AND WOULD like to get rid of your burden of guilt, you will first find that understanding much of what I already covered in Chapter 2 will give you some relief but not enough. To get over self-blame completely, you still need to know something about how all emotional disturbances are created and how each one of them can be eliminated.

How You Really Get Upset

Most people have the idea that we become disturbed in one of two ways. They believe that rough conditions in their lives or unhappy events make them disturbed. Or they believe that a person who has something wrong with himself physically cannot help being upset.

I have news for you. The major reason we get upset is that we talk ourselves into it. Our thoughts are the troublemakers that make us neurotic, not our parents, husbands or wives, or bosses. It is not a flat tire that gives you a fit of temper. It is the thought you are having as you open the car door and put your foot on the snow-covered highway and realize that you are in for a tough and rough time getting that tire changed. It is the way we talk to ourselves that keeps us cool or hot. This is called the ABC Theory of Emotions and goes like this:

There are two kinds of pain that we can experience. The first is a physical pain, and the other an emotional pain. If I throw a knife at your chest, and I call the knife A and the wound in your chest C, you will surely agree that A caused C, the knife caused the wound in the chest. Or if a car breaks your leg, the car is A and the broken leg C. The car broke your leg, or A caused C. This is always true of physical pain, even when you hurt yourself. Something has happened to your body which you can easily see and which usually comes from others. The skin is bruised, bones are broken, or blood is spilled.

Often we are in pain but cannot show any blood, broken bones, or bruised skin. Where does it come from? From B, the thoughts you have about A. It is your thinking that hurts you, not the things others have done or said about or to you. Suppose that someone calls you a nasty name. The name-calling is A. You then tell yourself something like: "Oh, isn't that horrible, he doesn't like me. I can't stand it." That is the sort of thing we all often do at B. The next thing we notice is a feeling of anger, or a headache, or a feeling of depression at C, in our bodies. We are inclined to think that the nasty words made us upset, when in fact it was our thinking about the words that hurt us. A does not cause us emotional pain, B does.

The thoughts that upset us at B are called irrational ideas. All of us have a number of irrational beliefs that cause us trouble but that we nevertheless believe in very strongly. We have been so trained to think irrationally, stupidly, and nonsensically that we will be quite surprised, as we continue to read, at how much nonsense we hold sacred. Albert Ellis, Ph.D., the clinical psychologist who developed his school of psychotherapy called

58

rational-emotive therapy, has listed about a dozen common irrational notions that can cause practically any and all neurotic symptoms.

If you really want to stop being depressed, angry, or nervous, you will first have to see the common sense in the notion that you always upset yourself. Then you will have to discover just what irrational ideas you continually feed yourself. And finally you will have to think through that mess and come to see how you believe in trash and that more sensible ideas should replace the stuff you have been feeding yourself.

Try to understand just what I am saying. My point is that no one at any time in any place can upset you in any way unless you allow it. Being imperfect, you will of course not be able to fight your neurotic tendencies all the time. But it is amazing how successful you can be if you know how you upset yourself and what you will have to do to calm down. I have seen this work nicely with scores and scores of persons who were disturbed persons most of their lives and who learned how to be largely undisturbed once they were shown how. At first they often thought I was the nutty one because of the strange things I told them. You will admit that it sounds very strange. Think about it and I am sure that you will sooner or later see how much sense it makes. But you must work very hard at changing your present thinking into sensible thinking. If you have happy thoughts, you will feel happy. If you have unangry thoughts, you will feel unangry. And if you do not think fearful thoughts, nothing in the world is going to make you feel afraid.

In the past when we have been disturbed, we have always insisted that something or someone in our lives had to change. This is wrong. Often those around us or the situation in which we live cannot or will not change. This does not need to doom us to a life of misery. We can still keep our cool even if the situation or the person does not change. Thank God for small favors. Just imagine what living would be like if it weren't that way. It would mean that a woman with an alcoholic husband had no choice but to be depressed until he stopped drinking. And suppose he never stopped his boozing. Why, she would have to be positively miserable all her life. That's nonsense. We *can* change for the better even if others or bad conditions never change. All we need to do is change our thinking at B and our feelings about A will change very dramatically at C.

The Irrational Ideas of the Self-blamer

Depression by self-blame is never caused because we have failed, because we have sinned, or because we accidentally hurt someone. Instead, self-blame depression is caused at B because we believe that (1) we must be perfect or that (2) people are bad and should be severely blamed. These are two irrational notions that always cause us to be depressed if we think of them and believe in them when we have done wrong.

I have explained in Chapter 2 why it is foolish to think that you have to be perfect and I have explained why you are never a bad person even though you have behaved badly. If you challenge these two notions hard enough, you will find yourself level-headed and quite undepressed even when you are quite guilty of a number of acts. But you must talk vigorously to yourself or it just won't work.

First, notice that you do indeed say this hogwash just before you become depressed. If you don't notice it at first, slow down your thinking and try to catch yourself in the act. It may take some practice, but sooner or later you are almost certain to hear out loud some of the neurotic things you have been saying at B for years.

A lady came to me once quite depressed after having an argument with her husband. It seems that her husband would find a legitimate fault in her behavior, she would argue in her defense but still wind up quite depressed. I suggested that she blamed herself over the real faults he pointed out because no one is any good unless one is faultless. At first she was not able to hear herself think these thoughts, but after several weeks of weekly sessions she came to her next appointment saying: "I'm beginning to see what you mean. Why, all week I could suddenly hear myself say the most awful things to myself. And they were all bad, all self-condemning, all mean things about myself. No wonder I'd get depressed. Why, the tongue-lashing I've been giving myself would make anyone depressed."

Do not be misled about these self-verbalizations. They always precede your feelings even if you can't recall a single thought you had before becoming depressed. The fact that your mind may seem as though it is blank doesn't change a thing. You *did* say something neurotic to yourself if you now feel upset. Accept that on faith for the moment and then start practicing listening to yourself *as* you get upset. Remember, your brain is never asleep even when you are. It is like the heart. It never stops until you are dead. During sleep you are thinking in the form of symbols just as your feelings express your irrational thoughts during the day.

Next, after you convince yourself that your moods come from your thinking, you must then convince yourself of just how wrong that thinking really is. To do this you must do the same thing you did as a child when you got rid of your childhood superstitions. Stop and think for a moment how much nonsense you were taught as a kid but no longer believe. You once believed that black cats caused bad luck, a broken mirror was supposed to make your life miserable for seven years, and dark rooms were dangerous because they were filled with ghosts. Do you believe in these superstitions today? I doubt it. If you do, you are sicker than you realize and should get yourself to a psychotherapist immediately. Assuming that you no longer believe in that hogwash, ask yourself the question, "How did I rid myself of those beliefs even though most children believed the same nonsense?" You will discover that as you grew older you could think more clearly about spooks and stuff like that and you soon talked yourself out of accepting those beliefs any longer. Notice now, you are not afraid of these things today because the spooks have gone away or because you no longer break mirrors. And you still have cats crossing your path. In other words, A has not changed over the years. But C (your fears) has changed. Why? Obviously the only element that has changed is B, the way you think of A, that is, cats, mirrors, and ghosts. The moment you believed that those beliefs were stupid beliefs, that was the moment you got rid of your fear. The change in attitude is the ingredient that brings this about.

How do we change our long-standing attitudes and beliefs? The same way we changed our belief in Santa Claus. Only by thinking very carefully about Santa Claus, by stopping to ask yourself how reasonable it is to think so-and-so, were you able to undo your belief in that myth. It was not simply a matter of your growing older that made you give up your belief in Santa, it was your tendency to question as you aged along with the help of your friends who also questioned as they grew older. You

62

must have asked yourself such questions as: "How could Santa get all the material he needs way up there at the North Pole where there are no trees, no roads, no gas stations, no factories, no paint shops, and so on? How could he possibly make enough toys in one year to supply presents for all the kids in the whole world? It takes the whole world a year to do that, so how can one man with a band of elves do the same? Even if he could, how could he possibly know what every child wanted? He would have to be a god to make enough toys, and no one ever called him that! Assuming that he could even do that, how could one man get around the world in one night? With reindeers, not a jet. And they fly yet! Who has ever seen a reindeer fly? And if he is supposed to come down the chimney, what does he do if some are too small, or if a house doesn't have one at all? And wouldn't he be so filthy after a bit that the soot would choke him?" And so on and so on.

It is this kind of challenging and *nothing else* which changed your attitudes. Time has nothing directly to do with it at all, as you can plainly see if you go into the hills and hear how folk there are still plenty afraid of ghosts, how natives of the Caribbean islands still stick pins into dolls to kill their enemies, and how witchcraft is practiced throughout the world in the backward places. They do not stop and analyze their beliefs, so they go on blindly believing them.

It is through this same process that you have changed drastically some of the most forceful prejudices of childhood. Wasn't there a time when the thought of being naked before the opposite sex was shocking? Don't tell me that you don't undress before your spouse these days? Didn't you think that you wanted to be a cowboy or a fireman when you were a youngster but wouldn't think of it today? Haven't you changed your political views over the years? All these beliefs were held most staunchly once upon a time but were surely changed over the years because you rethought them, examined them, analyzed them, and seriously questioned them. *That* is what made them change. If you can rethink and question long-standing ideas like the above, you can rethink and question the irrational teachings that were taught to you. All you have to do is think very thoroughly about the reasons you must be perfect, why everyone has to like you, or how can people really hurt you if they say unkind things to you. Think over those ideas and several others, throw them out of your head, change them into sane ideas, and you will rid yourself of more neurotic baggage than you can believe.

Though Rejected, You're Still O.K.

One of the reasons people dread being rejected is their belief that the rejection means that they are no good, that they would not have been rejected had they been different, and that the rejection is proof of their worthlessness. According to this view, the person doing the rejection is always right and superior, while the one rejected is always in the wrong and is somehow faulty.

But is this correct? Why isn't there something wrong with the fellow who rejects me? Can't he be all screwed up and passing judgment on me based on his own weaknesses, jealousies, and prejudices? When you stop and realize that every single soul who ever lived and is living and will live is neurotic some of the time, how can you continue to think that every judgment made by those neurotics out there must be accurate judgments? It seems to me that this is the first lesson we must all make about the evaluations of others: Others can be petty, prejudiced, mean, and envious. Their rejection of you tells you more about them than about you. For example, if your friend goes to the grocery counter and buys grapes, peaches, and bananas, but doesn't buy apples, what is he telling you about apples? That apples are bad? That no one else will approve of apples? That apples should feel ashamed of themselves and break down and have a depression? Quite the contrary! Your friend's rejection of apples only tells us that *he* finds them distasteful and prefers other fruit. Other people will surely find these same apples quite satisfying. The grocer has only to be patient and wait for other customers. In short, you have learned a lot about your friend's *tastes* but nothing at all about apples.

And isn't it the same if your friend rejects you? He may not like your political views, but that hardly proves that your views are wrong, does it? He may not like your looks any longer, such as your shoulder-length hair. Again, that says nothing about you, only about his prejudices. You might, of course, want to think over his criticism and decide whether he is correct in his criticism and get your hair cut. But you could also decide that his is wrong and let him go his way. Or if his friendship is very important to you, then cutting your hair to please him might be a sensible compromise with yourself, provided it did not bother you too much. In any event, his rejection of you might or might not be fair if you focus on the *thing* about you that he does not like. But it is never correct to conclude that his rejection of you is fair if he means that you are completely no good as a human being. Even if everyone you know rejects you, that still is no proof of your value as a human being. Thousands of people rejected Martin Luther King. Thousands rejected

Jesus, for that matter. But this hardly means that these two men were bad or worthless.

Instead of getting "all shook up" over an occasional rejection, the wise person can try to win that approval back, or, if this seems pointless, he can accept the fact that he is only a human being who can never please everyone and get busy finding people with whom he is compatible. This is particularly good advice where one's love life is concerned. I can't tell you how many people I have worked with who turned mushy inside just because someone they loved rejected them. Sure, it's not nice to be disapproved of, but it's hardly life and death. In every case in which I have been successful in getting the rejected one to understand the reason for the rejection and asked him to improve that aspect of himself for which he was rejected (if it could be improved) and then urged him to find new people to relate to—in every case in which this has been done the rejection was soon forgotten or reduced in significance, was used to good advantage, and other persons were found with whom the individual got along quite well.

This is what I am referring to when I say, "Be kind to yourself." Put yourself on a higher plane. Value yourself even if others don't, and you may be surprised at how people will think more of you. Those people with a healthy sense of respect, who don't let an occasional rejection throw them, have fewer rejections to deal with than those who are always getting depressed because of a disapproval and who then try so hard to prevent the next rejection that they try too hard to please others. They strain for approval and stand on their psychological heads to be loved. This will cool off more people than they ever suspect. People can sense when you are desperate for approval and it makes them uncomfortable. In addition, they wonder what is wrong with you that you have to try so hard to please them.

Expect Setbacks

As you come to understand what is depressing or disturbing you, there may be some improvement fairly quickly because you are trying hard, you are highly motivated, and any advice that sounds as though it might help you is latched on to.

A second phase usually sets in at this point in which the old symptoms reappear and it seems as though no progress has been made. To understand these setbacks you must think of your behavior as a complicated set of habits. You all know how habits are. You don't need to think about them at all. You can drive your car through a town and have your thoughts on something else at the same time. Miles after you leave the town you wake up and wonder if you came to that town yet. That is an example of how beautifully habits work for us.

Neurotic behavior can be learned just as well, but the results of being controlled by neurotic habits are much more unpleasant. Trying to change any habit usually requires great energy over a period of time and you must always expect failures. Making typing errors, smoking cigarettes, getting to bed late: these are all common habits and we all know how tough it can be to overcome them. Imagine how much more difficult it is to overcome a habit such as being afraid of people, remaining silent in a group, being lazy and goofing off, running yourself down. Yes, these are habits too. And when you try to undo them you can be sure that you will have plenty of slips. That is to be expected. Habits can be overcome only through much work and after numerous failures. Remember the last part of that sentence. I knew a man once who mishandled funds in the organization he worked for because he needed some ready cash and because it was a quick way to solve his problems. He also had a habit of lying his way out of a fix if he was questioned about his money-juggling. That was another bad habit. As such he should have expected that he would steal again and lie again even though he was in counseling and even though he had not done either of the above in months. Since it was a habit, there was every reason to believe that if he got in a financial bind again, the habitual thing for him to do would be to embezzle money and wiggle his lying way out of it.

This does not mean that everyone has to repeat his symptoms after they are once under control. It only means that we get sloppy with what we have learned and that this permits the old habits to grow stronger over the days and weeks. And before we know it we have gone and done the same thing again which always gave us trouble.

Be kind to yourself. Understand habits, their favorable and their unfavorable sides. And the next time you repeat some dumb piece of behavior after you thought you had it whipped, forgive yourself and realize how you were the victim of a habit. But then get on the ball and fight the thing by thinking it out sensibly as you did before, which enabled you to gain the healthy control in the first place.

This is also extremely important for people to understand who are frustrated by the annoying behavior of others. A husband who habitually comes home late for supper is certain to do the same after a period of time even though you had a big quarrel over it yesterday, even though he promises to improve, and, yes, even though he has been doing better for a number of days. Habit is likely to have its way. If you kindly but firmly talk about the issue instead of fume over it, he can get quicker control over his habit the second time around, he won't be using his efforts to blame himself or you, and he can quietly analyze how the habit began to creep up on him again.

Some persons insist that the husband or the wife immediately return for more counseling the first time an old habit reappears. This is not necessary. I always try to assure my clients and their spouses or parents that the client is almost certain to slip sometime and that he cannot help it. In fact, I try to inform both parties of this likelihood before our counseling ends. If both understand this fully, it is amazing how much worry, anger, and depression is avoided because no one is making mountains out of molehills, no one is blaming someone else, and most important, the guilty party is not blaming himself.

You Are *Not* Your Actions

One of the main reasons we have setbacks is that it is so easy for us to think of ourselves and our behavior as being the same. Logical thinking practically seems to scream out that we must judge ourselves by our actions. It goes against everything that sounds reasonable not to rate ourselves by our accomplishments, our financial successes, our conquests, and our popularity. So, when our behaviors stink we are likely to feel the old neurotic habit take hold and we have a setback.

Not rating ourselves is such a difficult thing, however, that we should look at and study the matter much more deeply so that we really understand the need to accept ourselves when we behave badly and talk ourselves out of the usual self-blame.

When you hate yourself because of a bad act, you are actually making a number of rash statements. Suppose you say something offensive at a party and turn a few people against you. Among the thoughts you could and are likely to have are: "Gee, I spoke rudely to John." (True.) "I'm always saying dumb things just to get attention." (False. No one always makes dumb or rude comments, just some of the time, and usually very infrequently at that.) "I'll never learn to watch my p's and q's." (False. How do you know what you will be doing in the future? Are you a fortune-teller? Are you a mystic? If so, write me and we'll make millions at the racetrack.) What usually happens is that you believe that you are the biggest dunce in the world, and *then*, because you have convinced yourself of the hopelessness of it all, you fail to make the necessary effort to change, so you don't change. Then you pat yourself on the back for making so many correct predictions. You haven't predicted at all. You *forced* things to come out the way you convinced yourself they had to come out.

So if you are not always being tactless, why should you hate yourself all the time? Before you made your rude remark, and after it too, you did a number of charitable things. You opened the car door for your wife. You helped your hostess with her chair at the dinner table. You took home the baby-sitter that night. If bad acts make you bad, then shouldn't good acts make you good? If so, to find out if you are a decent human or not, just keep score each day and you will see that your kindnesses far outnumber your blunders.

At this point you are likely to protest that one can hardly give oneself a star just for opening a door for

70

someone or for taking home the baby-sitter. I disagree. Just stop and think for a moment what you would think of your behavior if you let the baby-sitter walk home two miles in the dark by herself. Wouldn't this be something else you could crucify yourself for? Then why not like yourself for doing a nice thing if you would definitely dislike yourself if you didn't do it?

The point I am making is that most of the time you actually do behave decently, only you don't think about it. It is only when you behave less than perfectly that you take notice of your actions and get angry with yourself.

Perhaps another argument against rating yourself by your actions is the impossibility of describing all of you by a few bad actions. If you are an alcoholic and cause trouble to others because of that, are we to believe that your alcoholic habit describes you completely? You still bring home the bread. You don't shoot people on the street. You are a loyal member of a political party, a church, and a business. To say that all of you is worthless because part of you is deficient is like saying you should be shot if you have bad eyes, or stutter, or have a fear of elevators. Is a whole house worthless because its roof leaks? Is a new car ready for the junk pile because it has a flat tire?

No one in his right mind would take such views. He would always separate the leak in the roof from the house as a whole. And he would immediately change the flat tire rather than junk the car. In both instances the part would be separated from the whole and not used to describe the whole. It is the same with human beings. We all have faults and I refuse to believe that I'm all no good just because parts of me are no good.

And lastly, even if you think your actions and you are

the same, then why aren't the actions of children the same as the children? When a baby throws up on your lovely sofa you make one judgment about the vomiting and another judgment about the child (I hope). Don't tell me that you go around all day hating your children for the millions of irritating things they do. If you do, you are an ignorant and disturbed parent and are sure to raise neurotic children. But most of us have sense most of the time to separate the child from his behavior and not rate him by his noise, disorder, mess, and fighting. We love him through the whole thing even though there is much at times we don't like about him.

If we think this is rational in the case of children, why should it be any different with adults? Because we, as adults, should know better? Of course not! That takes us back to the comments I have already made that we are not perfect because we are human and that we will all misbehave for reasons of stupidity, ignorance, or disturbance.

Learn How to Debate with Yourself

Some of my clients have been so brainwashed into believing their irrational beliefs that they find it mighty hard to talk and challenge themselves out of believing this stuff. I have already advised you of the necessity to think about the reasonableness of your statements and shown you how you can change them if you analyze them carefully. Sometimes, however, more is needed. I can offer two other suggestions to help you change a sick attitude into a healthy one.

First, ask other people what they think about your beliefs. But make sure you ask a number of them who are not bothered by the same kind of problems. If you ask a depressive how he deals with failure, you will only get back the same nonsense you have already been feeding yourself, and that will tend to reinforce your neurotic thinking, not weaken it. Instead, get around a few people who handle failure and depression better than you do and ask their thoughts on the matter. We are usually persuaded somewhat by the crowd, so use that power to help you over your hang-up. This is a strong weapon, because we are all influenced by group pressures somewhat. If you live in a neighborhood of Republicans, you will surely find your own views changing slowly in that direction. If most of your male friends are wearing bell-bottom trousers, you will surely find yourself approving of them in time. The best example of group pressure that I can think of, however, is this business of long hair. First the teen-agers started it, then the younger adults picked it up, so did the entertainment people, and finally its influence was noticed even among members of the Senate and among the presidential candidates.

So move in different circles, associate with persons who have the values which you want but which you haven't managed to adopt yet, and I can assure you that some change in your thinking will probably follow.

The second important technique you can use to change your thinking along with analyzing your thinking is to say the *rational* thought aloud (if you are alone), or think it to yourself if you are not alone. Even if you don't believe the thought, think it anyway. Before you can believe an idea it must at least be in your head. You must hear how it sounds to you. Your irrational thought must be given some opposition even if it is half-hearted.

Haven't you ever tried on an article of clothing certain you wouldn't like it? You have done the same with food

73

which you were sure you wouldn't like but which you did like once you tasted it a few times. And aren't there a number of people you learned to like despite the fact that you had an aversion toward them initially? You might have asked the Smiths over because your preferred couple was busy one weekend. And to your surprise you found some good qualities in them you would not have realized had you not at least given them a halfhearted chance.

It is no different with our thoughts. If we try them on for size, we may be surprised how well they fit. So say sensible things to yourself when you are getting upset even though you are not totally convinced of them. The next time you put yourself down for making a mess of things fight those words with, "No, I'm still acceptable to myself even if I wasn't perfect on the job." You may then be inclined to say: "Quit fooling yourself, you jerk. You flubbed up royally and cost the company a wad of dough. It would serve you right if you got canned." Then whether you believed yourself or not, say something like: "I am not a bum because I goofed up. Mistakes will happen and who knows whether I won't learn a lot from this mistake. Even if the company doesn't want me, by golly I want me. I'm all I've got." And so on. You may be surprised that these sensible and charitable ideas may begin to grow on you because you are *at least listening to them.* If you don't even give them that much of a chance, how do you ever expect to believe them at all?

The whole process will, or at least should, resemble an exciting debate. You take both sides. In the beginning your neurotic voice is louder and more convincing. At the surface, however, you are debating those long-held views in a less convincing voice. You must debate with

yourself until the surface ideas grow in strength and
place the deeper ideas. When you utter an irratio[nal]
belief, give it some opposition with a rational bel[ief].
Never let irrational beliefs go unchecked. Always gi̇v̇e
each of them an antagonist. Tit for tat. Spend as much
time debating with yourself as you spend on blaming
yourself and you will be in clear water.

A further argument which you can always use to convince yourself that your neurotic ideas deserve to be
seriously debated is the fact that they have made you
neurotic. Do you need more proof? If your ideas and
beliefs were so sound, why would you be reading this
book? If you were such a wonderful example of Mr. or
Ms. Mental Health of 1972, then how is it you get so
depressed, or worried, or hostile at times? Like it or not,
dear reader, your present methods just aren't working
or you would be feeling great most of the time. If you
are in some kind of emotional disturbance most of the
time, then don't tell *me* how right and proper your attitudes and philosophies are. If they don't work for you,
why should they work for me? This is what usually
amuses me in counseling, especially in my groups. I have
had as many as half a dozen clients, all failures at self-
composure, argue and yell at me and all insisting that *I*
must be wrong about how to stay calm, when each and
every one of them was there because *they* couldn't keep
their cool.

Therefore, don't spend a lot of time assuming that I
must be nuts just because I sound different. Assume that
you must be screwy, or why would you have been suffering so much for so long? Do you argue with your
piano teacher? You are a conceited ass if you do. And
frankly, you are a stupid ass if you argue with your
psychotherapist. This doesn't mean that you shouldn't

75

ask questions and debate with him. That is the only way you will ever learn anything new and get your mind changed. But if you believe that you can never be wrong and that the expert is all wet, then you don't even get into a debate. Your mind is made up and you won't even give a new idea a chance. That is when you are being stupid. It was for this reason that I urged you in remarks above to say the proper thoughts to yourself even if you did not believe them. That shows you to be somewhat open to new possibilities, and from there who knows how far you can go? Only by using the above advice will you ever be able to accept such revolutionary ideas as: there are no bad people in the world, only bad deeds; no one can upset us emotionally, only physically; everyone has the right to be wrong and should not be condemned for his wrongdoing; and so on. Work at it and make it work!

4

Poor Me!

IF YOU HAVE EVER FELT SORRY FOR YOURSELF, YOU ARE already familiar with the second major cause of the blues: self-pity. Strange as it may seem, this method can crush you every bit as badly as guilt can. You cannot tell by looking at a depressive in which way he is depressing himself. The reasons for being tearful can be as different as night from day, but the end result is practically the same. Only in its extreme form does depression from guilt really take on a different character from depression by self-pity or depression by other-pity. For example, extreme guilt reactions sometimes cause people to punish themselves with knives, razor blades, cigarettes, etc., something not usually seen in the other forms of depression, especially other-pity.

If you suspect that you might be a self-pitier, face it. Too many people feel so guilty about being self-pitiers that they never see their own dynamics. I suppose the reason is that self-pity is associated with immaturity, the childish manipulation of others, and takes on the characteristics of the hysterical female.

Be that as it may, it is still in your best interests to consider the possibility that you mope around all the time because you feel sorry for yourself. If you cannot conclude that you are blaming yourself for something or that you are breaking your heart over someone else's troubles, then you can be reasonably sure that you are pitying yourself. Hard medicine to swallow perhaps! If you fight this insight, you will simply get nowhere. You will waste your time or the time of your counselor much as one of my clients once did because she simply could never face the fact that she was a first-class self-pitier. I constantly agreed with her in that she had suffered a most unfortunate event in her family life and could see no rational reason why in heaven's name it should have happened to someone like her. She had always run her life above suspicion, been charitable to all whom she contacted, harmed no one, and then her fiancé and favorite sister died on her within a half year of each other.

There was no reason why she would have felt guilty over these events, and although she was partially depressed over feeling sorry for the deceased, she could easily see that they were beyond suffering and safely in heaven. So that could not have been the major reason for her lengthy and deep feelings of despair. When I suggested that she felt sorry for herself because this lousy world had treated her completely unfairly, she protested so strongly that I was actually taken aback. I had never seen such unwillingness to consider oneself a self-pitier. Needless to say, this roadblock slowed us up for weeks. This observation, and many more of a similar nature, has led me to conclude that if you are not sure how you are depressing yourself, take a guess and look at self-pity very closely.

Two Thoughts Bring On Self-pity

Whenever you attempt to understand your self-pitying moods always ask yourself what you were thinking of immediately before you became upset. Then, of all the thoughts you can recollect, analyze and sort out those which make sense and those which do not. If you do this correctly, you will practically always come to the point where you have made the following two statements over some issue or event in your life: (*a*) I want my way in this matter and (*b*) it's awful if I don't get my way.

The first thought is a reasonable one and can never cause you any serious harm. As long as you want, desire, prefer, or wish for anything, you will never be upset if you don't get what it is you desire. All of you have already wished for a million things you have not received and it hasn't hurt one bit even though it may have left you slightly saddened. Haven't you wanted to be the president of the United States? Haven't you wanted to be a movie star, to be rich, to be famous, to write the great American novel, or to be the world's champion belly dancer? And hasn't this been a pleasant daydream even though it never seems to want to come true? As long as you take your desires with a grain of salt you won't get depressed if they don't materialize. It is only when you think that you *must* be right, when you believe that it is the *end of the world* not to have your dream yacht on the Mediterranean, and when you feel that it is positively *awful* if you aren't elected as the next secretary of the local P.T.A., that you begin to be upset.

Understand this thoroughly: you do not *need* a great deal in this life, and in fact you do not even *need* to live. Let's look at that first thought. All you need for life is food, shelter, and clothing. More than this makes living very nice but hardly essential. It is wonderful to have friends, but you will not die if you do not have

79

them. You could always become a hermit. However, it is unlikely that you will ever have to go that far because there will always be someone around who will sell you some bread and rent you a room. You could die without the bread or the room, but you certainly are not going to die if you break up with one or more of your close friends. What you do have to be careful of is that people don't *hate* you so very much that they are likely to shoot you on the street or not sell you food, etc. It is people's hatred, not their love, you should be *very* much concerned with.

The second thought, that you do not need to live, is easily proved when you stop to think of the numerous instances when you would voluntarily sacrifice your life for someone you loved or didn't even know. You would risk your life for your family, for your country, for someone who seemed to be drowning, or for someone in a burning building calling for help. Countless heroic acts have been performed by people who obviously believed that they did not consider life all that essential or they never would have risked it. Yet these same people might have been depressed the previous day because they thought that it was the end of the world when their jobs folded up or when they were told they had cancer.

Distinguishing Between Sadness and Tragedy

Another way of looking at these ideas is to see them as a confusion between what you think of as being sad and what you think of as being tragic. There are a great many happenings in your life that are sad, but only a few of them are tragic (even here, many tragedies would hardly be so tough on you if you viewed them differently).

Sad events give us feelings of regret and disappointment. These are not devastating emotions. We experience them often, with no ill effects, and they often don't last very long. But tragedies—now that is a different story. When we believe that we have been stricken with a catastrophe we usually cannot respond calmly to it.

Most of our self-pity depression comes because we confuse sad events with catastrophic or tragic events. That is, we honestly believe that what we are experiencing is *awful,* the *end of the world,* and simply *unbearable.* But is it? Where is the proof that something is awful? Who says it is? If you didn't listen to the overly sympathetic statements of your well-meaning friends, or to your own catastrophizing statements, do you suppose for a minute that you would be so upset? Not in a million years. You have to *talk* yourself into thinking that an event is unbearable, and most of the time (about 99 percent) you are dead wrong. The greatest majority of events in our lives are regrettable, not awful; are disappointing, not catastrophic; are sad, not tragic. If we unthinkingly talk or think ourselves into believing that something is awful, catastrophic, or tragic, we will, in the immediate moments following this kind of thinking, become blue and tearful. But if we correctly see that so many things which happen to us are only regrettable, disappointing, and sad, we will simply be mildly unhappy for a short time and then come back to a normal and optimistic mood.

Jim returned from the senior prom with his best girl only to be told by her that she wanted to break up. He immediately went into a tailspin and saw me the next day, very depressed. After hearing the facts, I could easily determine that something *sad* had happened to the young man (his girl friend was rejecting him) and that he had reacted to this surprising news by making a tragedy out of it (I'll die if I can't have her love).

In only one session Jim was shown how he was pitying himself and what he would have to do to stop this depression.

"It isn't because your girl is rejecting you that you're so blue, Jim," I protested. "It's because you think it's awful to be rejected."

"But it is. I didn't sleep all night wondering what I had done to turn her against me and wondering what I would do from now on."

"No, Jim, that's not why you're upset. Reviewing your behavior concerning your girl made good sense. You can't get depressed by trying to learn from your mistakes. Self-pity comes only when you think you must have something and that it's terrible and unbearable if you don't get it. In this case you were telling yourself that you still wanted to be sweethearts with the girl, and had you stopped there, you would have felt just sad and nothing more. But you went farther and convinced yourself that being rejected was unfair, that it was a terrible thing to do after all you had done for her, and that why did all this rotten stuff have to happen to you. When you believed these last ideas you wound up by eating your heart out and silently saying 'Poor me.'"

"But I did knock myself out for her, and now to be treated this way is very unfair."

"Sure it's unfair, but why shouldn't it be? Just because you don't want unfair things to happen to you does that mean they can't? Is it the end of the world just because you didn't get your way? Why couldn't you learn from this experience, consider it a pleasant memory, and go forth and woo a dozen new girl friends? You could do that fairly easily if you'd stop pitying yourself because she dumped you."

And so it went for the remainder of the session until he could see how he had made a mountain out of a mole-hill. The next time I saw him a week later he was completely over the blues and dating another girl! I attributed·his change to the fact that he easily saw how he had convinced himself that a sad event is no different from a tragic event. It is a lesson every self-pitier must learn if ho caros about hio mental health.

Disturbances Are Worse than Frustrations

Life is an endless series of frustrations. It is for this reason that the pro rather than the amateur in this business of living is not hell-bent on removing all his frustrations as a condition for a happy life. No one can go through even so much as one day without being somewhat frustrated (not having everything his own way). So he wisely works on being undisturbed first and then does what he can about reducing his frustrations. If he is successful in removing his problems and annoyances, well and good. He will have nothing to disturb himself over. But if he is unsuccessful in eliminating his frustrations, he can still be a reasonably happy person by not disturbing himself *over* the frustrations. In other words it is not necessary to be unfrustrated to be undisturbed. The only persons who do not experience frustrations are up in heaven or in the grave. The rest of us live persons cannot escape these displeasures any more than we can escape illness, taxes, or death. To be alive means to be frustrated. Therefore, to seek a life without frustration is like asking to die. So let's be satisfied to have these constant pains in the neck but learn at last how to roll with the punches.

If you do not distinguish between frustrations and disturbances, you will do two things that can hurt you very much. On the one hand, you will be making matters infinitely worse by adding the pain of the disturbance to the pain of the frustration, and on the other hand, you will be so screwed up from the disturbance that you won't be able to figure out a way to remove the frustration.

Take the case of Fred, a once-popular boy until he went off to the university. His classmates didn't know he was such a hotshot, so they treated him like the rank and file instead of as a leader. This got to his ego, but badly, and Fred soon felt so sorry for himself that he became depressed. He began to doubt his worthwhileness and was soon keeping to himself. The loss of recognition naturally continued until Fred took an overdose of drugs and nearly died. This brought him immediately into the limelight and for a time he was the talk of the dorm. But even this petered out in a matter of days and left Fred unrecognized once more. Again he turned this into a catastrophe and thought he had to do something desperate to catch the attention of the school. So Fred deliberately got drunk and had an accident. His name was read over the television news, and his arrest was the talk of the campus for a time. When the dust settled and Fred was back in school he found things worse than ever. By now his associates sized him up for a screwball and had even less to do with him than before. After a couple of other attention-getting accidents, Fred figured he had had it and thought it was time to get some help. Not only was he still lonely and depressed but he had lost time in school, had injured himself several times, and had collected a police record to boot.

This is what I mean by a disturbance being worse than a frustration. Had Fred not made so much of being an unknown student and had he allowed his normal talents to thrust him upward in the eyes of his peers, eventually he could have regained a position of prestige and leadership. Instead, Fred believed that to be unknown was a fate worse than death, that he simply could not stand being unpopular, and that any course of action was justified to correct this frustration. So he proceeded to hurt himself infinitely more than his being unpopular was hurting him. In addition, while he was in the grips of this neurosis, he was actually unable to see how he was making matters worse and how by changing just a few moves in his strategy he could get practically all he wanted. However, a disturbed mind does not think in clear terms, so Fred went from bad to worse until therapy stepped in and showed him how he was incorrectly believing that not being a big wheel on campus was terrible, that he ought to feel sorry for himself and get everyone else to feel the same way, and that being frustrated was the worst of all fates, even worse than being upset.

Self-pity from False Accusations

Most people take criticism very poorly. They feel so pained and lose so much sleep over the unkind remarks and insults of others that a thorough knowledge of how to handle this situation is needed if they are going to keep their wits about them and avoid another occasion for being blue.

The next time you are accused of anything, you can avoid being disturbed over it if you will ask yourself two questions: "Is it true?" or, "Is it false?" In the event you decide that it is true, do not blame yourself for being found guilty, since as a human being you have the right to be faulty. Suppose your husband calls you a tramp because you enjoy dancing with other men at parties. You mingle freely among the guests but he insists you are flirting, and he insists you stop. Instead of pitying yourself for being so misunderstood, simply examine his statement carefully and decide whether he is right or wrong.

Suppose you decide that he is right. Well and good. You have been a flirt. You have enjoyed leading the men on and you honestly have to agree that you would be plenty sore if your husband behaved as you do at parties. Now you have to convince yourself that you are not a bad person merely because you were thoughtless. You have a right to be wrong, and in fact you are grateful for your husband's telling you your behavior looks trampy, because you can then change it. Since you do not want to make such an unflattering impression at parties, you will try very hard to avoid this pattern in the future.

Notice how you have profited from being called a tramp instead of allowing yourself to become depressed? Quite an improvement, wouldn't you say?

Now suppose that after thinking his accusation over carefully you decide he is dead wrong. Why should you be disturbed over that? It is really only a matter of his opinion against yours. You surely don't become disturbed over every difference of opinion that you two have, so why should you make this an exception merely because you are now disagreeing about you? You need only tell yourself: "There he goes again, the poor dear. Every time I dance with another man he makes himself neurotically angry because he thinks I'm going to have an affair with every man I touch. I wonder what *his* problem is? Maybe he has too little confidence in his ability to keep me and this may be why he gets so scared when I'm not right beside him at all times. Well, that's his problem. He can't help it, and I surely didn't create it for him, so why should I get all shook up because he thinks I'm a tramp? I'm not one and if he thinks I am, he'll just have to decide what he wants to do about it."

It makes no difference what the accusation is. It can always be handled in a kindly and charitable way toward the person making the unkind remark if you always keep the above facts in mind. This also means that no one can insult you. No matter what they say about you, all you have to do to take the sting out of the remark is ask yourself whether the remark is true or false. An insult is something we do to ourselves. It is not something done to us by others. What they do is give us their opinions; what we do is make something personal out of it and get all insulted that others should have ideas in their heads that we disapprove of.

Recently a member of one of my groups said that she was highly insulted the previous night because a man propositioned her rather brazenly in the presence of her husband. Needless to say, the husband was incensed and ready for a fight. But I insisted that they had insulted themselves and that they needn't have taken the fellow's remarks so personally. For one thing, she was probably not the only woman he ever thought of propositioning, so why should she think it was only she that he was singling out? Secondly, he was really being flattering to make such a suggestion, since there are probably many women he would never think of asking for such favors. Thirdly, was he actually hurting anyone with his crude ways? The poor sap must have been terribly insensitive to make such a boner in the first place, or he must have been terribly lonely and desperate to come on like a bull in a china closet. One should have sympathy and compassion for anyone who is hurting that much. And instead of taking a swing at the fellow or feeling insulted, how much more sensible it would have been for my client to say, "No, thanks," to the fellow, that she appreciated his kind thought and that her husband must surely be flattered by it as well. She could have ended by wishing him good hunting! Wouldn't that have been an achievement for mental health?

Avoiding Depression Over an Unfaithful Spouse

There are generally two typical reactions to the discovery that your spouse has committed adultery. The first is that you have let your partner down and you feel terribly guilty about it. The second is self-pity because you don't know how you could be treated so shabbily after all the sacrifices you made for your beloved. Of course, after either of these initial reactions subsides, there is an upsurge of resentment and bitterness that can get amazingly furious.

I suggest that if you behave in either of these manners, you are being just plain silly and should seriously consider facing such an event in something like the following manner.

Be grateful that it was not you who had to resort to an affair. You at least had the willpower and fortitude to resist a flirtation, while your impulsive and dependent spouse could not do so. Aren't you proud of yourself for this accomplishment? And don't you have compassion for your lover because he or she could not resist temptation? That's right, take pride in your superior control. Remaining loyal isn't the easiest thing in the world by any means, especially these days. To keep your wedding vows takes fortitude not many people have.

What you have to see is that both of you had thought of having affairs numbers of times, and both of you had many opportunities to do so, but you were mature enough to stick by your promises. You showed your capacity for dependability and trust while your spouse failed in both of these vital areas of married life.

And if your spouse comes back at you with: "But I wouldn't have looked for an affair if you had only done this or that for me. It's your fault that I was driven into someone else's arms," don't swallow that stuff. Any day of the week you could pull out a list of complaints against your mate that can match his list against you. Still you did not let these gripes throw *you* off the path. You took him with all the faults and worked around them. You didn't use them as excuses for holding hands with someone behind the water cooler.

When you look at infidelity this way you will feel pride in yourself and compassion for your mate. You certainly can't feel depressed (*a*) if you aren't blaming yourself for not being the perfect mate and (*b*) if you aren't convincing yourself the sky has fallen in. An affair is usually nothing more than a serious message that something is wrong in the marriage. That something need hardly be you always. It could just as well be the partner.

One client I shall never forget had affairs for years and his wife knew it. She cursed herself that he always had to run with other women, thinking he was doing this because she was seriously lacking as a female. When she came to me in marital counseling she was quite depressed and had as low an opinion of herself as one can get. But all that changed when I convinced her that her husband ran around because he was a human alley cat and no matter what kind of wife she was it would never keep him home for long. I told him this one day when both of them were seeing me together and after a moment's thought he had to admit that it was absolutely true because he really could not find serious faults with his wife. In fact, the idea struck him as rather startling, so he eventually decided to divorce his wife and be honest with her for the first time in years. He simply liked catting around and had no intention of stopping. What he wanted from marriage was a maid, a cook, and a laundress. He decided that this was unfair to his wife, so he let her go to find another fellow who could live with her only.

Neurotics Often Slip

To spare you a lot of depression if you have a habit of pitying yourself, remember always that the behavior in others changes in a very uneven way. One day a person behaves admirably and maturely and the next day is right back to the same old tricks. This can be exasperating after you have not seen the annoying behavior for a time and you think that at last the person has conquered it.

If you are finally at peace with yourself because your child has stopped his stealing, brace yourself. If the right pressures come together, he can begin stealing again as though he had never had counseling and as though you hadn't made any dent in his pattern. If you are not careful at such times, you are likely to throw up your hands in desperation and catastrophize about how futile all your efforts have been and how you might just as well throw in the sponge.

This would be a serious mistake. This is not the time to get depressed. Remember that anything we learn tends to be forgotten with time. This applies to our behavior just as well as it does to the multiplication table. People get sloppy with their thinking if they aren't practicing rational thoughts. That is why an ex-alcoholic can start drinking again. That is why a child who hasn't stolen anything for a half year can suddenly start doing that again. And that is why you too can get depressed again even though you thought you understood how you get that way and haven't been really blue in a year. When we drop our guard we ask for trouble.

It is no different than in the case of dieting. Suppose that you came to me to lose weight and you learned to discipline yourself so well that you took off all the weight you wanted. Would that be the end of the story? Would that mean that you didn't have to diet and fight temptation constantly from then on? Of course it wouldn't. To keep the weight off, you would have to diet practically every day for the rest of your life. To remain undisturbed you must watch yourself or you will find yourself being angry, blue, or fearful. And to get out of that mood you would have to do the same things you did to gain calmness before.

A slip is hardly an awful thing and surely doesn't mean that no gains have been made at all. Gains are measured in three ways: frequency, duration, and severity.

Frequency: if your husband is now quarreling with you only once a week whereas he was doing so every day previously, he has made a significant gain. Be happy!

Duration: if his arguments last only an hour instead of all night, he has made a gain. Be happy!

Severity: if he only throws cups and saucers instead of putting his fist through the wall, he has made a gain. Be happy!

The idea that our nutty behavior will automatically stop when we have uncovered a long-forgotten memory which has supposedly been eating at our unconscious ever since childhood is Freudian mythology. Sometimes behavior stops wonderfully abruptly, but in the majority of cases it diminishes slowly, fading out gradually. Woe to the person who expects a flash of insight to make one's mate or child wake up a new person. That person is doomed to depression.

Self-pity Can Be a Powerful Weapon

Because practically everyone believes that he can be made upset by others or that he can upset others, it has occurred to millions of people to use this observation in controlling people. One of the best ways to control others is through guilt. If you show your friend how hurt you are because of something she said, you are hoping that she will feel bad over her remark and never treat you like that again. One sure way to convince her that she is a louse for what she did is to make a long face, cry a bit, and hope your self-pity crushes her. In all likelihood you will achieve your aim beautifully, since your friend will certainly blame herself for making you so blue.

This is a favorite technique of control used by neurotic mothers to keep their children from growing up. "Come home by eleven, Jenny," the mother says to her adult daughter. "You know how worried I get when you're not in. I can't sleep a wink while you're out."

Mamma wants Jenny to see her pain. That is what will bring Jenny home. If Jenny had any sense, she would say to her mamma: "I hope you won't worry about me, Mother. But if you insist on making yourself all nervous and depressed over my not being in early, then I suppose you'll just have to worry. You're the one who is upsetting you, not me. If that problem bothers you a great deal, I hope you'll go see someone about it."

I know that a great many readers will protest this as unkind treatment of the mother, totally devoid of respect for her tender concern. On the contrary. For Jenny to do otherwise is tantamount to making a neurotic worrier and depressive out of her mother. The more the girl accepts the responsibility for the mother's disturbance, the more the mother will tend to use her grief and anguish to get her way. How kind is that?

One of the most powerful ways in which self-pity is used is as a suicidal threat. When your boyfriend says to you, "Sally, marry me or I'll kill myself," he is feeling so sorry for himself that he hopes you will take pity upon him and agree to the marriage. The sorrier he feels, the better a chance he usually has for getting his way with those people who have a weak spot in their hearts for martyrs. The dangerous part of this practice is the fact that responding to this pity encourages it all the more. This could lead to further suicidal threats and perhaps eventually to a successful suicide!

No one knows just how many drug users and alcoholics get started on their habits out of a feeling of self-pity, but I would guess that the percentage is staggering and is much more than most authorities appreciate. I can speak more knowingly about alcoholics than addicts and in that area I am sure a great deal of drunkenness is for nothing else than to make someone feel guilty or sorry.

93

Just listen to the pack of fellows at a bar sometime and you will hear all the self-pity nonsense you can possibly swallow. A fellow may get drunk because the little woman was irritable or because she paid more attention to the dog than to him. Whatever the reason, it is fair to state that drinkers are not only a sorrowful lot, but usually feel sorry for themselves as well.

I do not wish to demean or be harsh on alcoholics, but I think the truth hurts less than ignorance. So let me say this: alcoholics and heavy drinkers are very often insecure fellows who cry in their beer because they don't get their way. Ever notice a child when he doesn't get what he wants? He often acts so hurt one would think the world was coming to an end. Why, to see what he goes through, you would think going to bed early was going to kill him. All the tears and screaming is self-pity, pure and simple, and it has one purpose: to work on *your* sense of pity for him so that you will give in.

What is involved in this situation is not only self-pity but other-pity as well. I shall be dealing with that in more detail in the next chapter, but for the present it is important to realize what power you give to others by playing into their self-pity techniques. I can think of a score of clients who have never grown up because they were such successful sympathy seekers. Why learn to accept things philosophically when all it takes to get your way is to appear crushed, scream your head off, show people what anguish you are in, and then keep this up until they say they are sorry?

I was recently reminded again just how deliberate all these self-pitying hysterics can really be. One young man called me on the phone and conversed for half an hour. He was as cool as you please, made good sense, and for all the world was on top of things. A couple of hours

94

later his father called from the local psychiatric ward to tell me that Junior was lying profusely and that I hadn't the foggiest notion of what was really happening to his son. It seems that only minutes after Junior called me, he had had a wild scene at home during which he acted so upset and off his rocker it was thought advisable to hospitalize him. Before agreeing to enter, however, Junior wanted to call me for advice. Again I was talking to the calmest, most contained, and sensible person I had talked to all day.

If you don't think that can confuse a therapist, try it sometime. What was happening, of course, was the calculated use by the boy of throwing an emotional fit merely to get sympathy and to force his parents to be so worried that they would be too scared to do anything drastic. Little did they realize how they were being sucked into his little game which in this instance backfired a wee bit.

Protecting Yourself from Becoming a Doormat

One of the unhealthiest consequences of pitying yourself is that you will allow people to use you, manipulate you, and take advantage of you. Countless millions of children and adults go through their lives licking their wounds, suffering in silence, crying in privacy, and feeling that they have no right to stand up for themselves.

The self-pitier goes along thinking he has no rights, believing that a confrontation with his spouse is worse than having high blood pressure or migraine headaches, and feeling for some mysterious reason that he must always be wrong whenever someone challenges his thinking. Underlying this sad state of affairs is a fear of thinking well of oneself, a fear of being selfish and self-centered. And there is some truth to this. But one must understand what is meant by selfishness. I regard some selfishness as perfectly sane and healthy. I don't like the use of the word "selfish," because it suggests wanting one's own way exclusively. That is an immature way to be and hardly worth recommending. But if we change that word and call it "enlightened self-interest," then we come closer to what all healthy people possess.

Look around you sometime and notice how the strong people in your life, in politics, where you work, all have a high degree of self-interest. They do not mind in the least standing up for their rights, arguing at some length if necessary, and breaking up relationships if that is what is called for. They do not take pushing around, because they do not feel sorry for themselves when injured. Instead, they feel indignant and immediately become assertive because *fair is fair*. This is the key to overcoming your tendency toward becoming a doormat. When you really feel that you have been fair in your dealings, don't give very much more or you will find yourself feeling abused and unappreciated. Some people just aren't going to play fair, because they honestly don't see what you are so unhappy about. You must tell them or write it out for them, or perhaps even show in your actions that you have had enough. Unless you do this, you will pity yourself, get depressed, and make your friend or spouse feel guilty or angry. You could, of course, continue your self-pity and carry it to extremes to get your way, but just think what it would cost you to win this way. Generally what happens when your self-pity doesn't work is that you finally have a confrontation, and for a time there is a change. As the days go by, however, there is a gradual reestablishment of the old pattern where you do all the dishes, spend evenings home alone while he is out with the boys, and so on.

96

To avoid this trap, remember that *no one steps on you without your allowing it.* You actually cooperate in a person's controlling you. The fact that you often complain and cause minor changes to be made does not change the fact that eventually things fall into their old pattern because you allow them to.

This happens because (*a*) you think too little of yourself, (*b*) you will do too much to preserve a relationship, since you think you will never get another one, or (*c*) both. Then the only thing you have left is the strangely dissatisfying feeling that no one understands you, that you will just have to suffer through life while others get their ways, and that just maybe someplace in heaven they have a very special place for martyrs.

Enough of this, friend! The time has come for you to let those around you know once and for all that you have had enough of their pushing around and unless they let up at once they will not get your cooperation any longer, and if need be, the relationship will dissolve. It might amaze you how quickly most people will start giving in when they truly see that you won't be bamboozled any longer.

I shall never forget the case of the mouse that roared. Ruth was a sheepish and bedraggled young divorcée. Her three children were her total responsibility and she was trying, with the help of welfare, to do a proper job of raising them, but she lived near her mother and sister. A boyfriend or two also entered the picture from time to time. Between these people and Ruth there was usually the most lopsided relationship I had ever seen. Ruth simply couldn't say, "No." Or rather, she *wouldn't* say, "No." Whatever mamma or sis asked of her she did. It mattered not that Ruth had work planned, or that she was tired running her own household, or that she needed help from others. All they had to do was suggest a favor and Ruth felt obliged to hop to and help out.

She kept her resentment to herself all through these episodes and wouldn't do anything to let the others know how irked she was. Naturally, in time she became quite depressed. When I saw her she looked like gloom itself. So I immediately tried to show her that being bossed by everyone was something she allowed because she was afraid of being rejected and afraid of hurting their feelings. I explained how rejection itself did not hurt persons unless they made a big thing of it, and hurting other people's feelings was impossible unless *they* allowed themselves to be hurt. I suggested that, instead of feeling sorry for herself because others could not see their unfairness, Ruth start by being fair to herself first and to let the chips fall where they may. If her sister or her mother disowned her for her independence, she would at least get them off her back, a not inconsequential relief. In all likelihood, however, I suspected that the more respect Ruth showed herself, the more respect she would gain from others.

The very next week she came to her session to report that she had turned down her sister's telephone request to baby-sit. It was difficult for her to do and she was quite nervous as she stood up for herself for the first time in years, but she stuck to her guns and politely hung up the phone. For the next several hours she was jittery and unsure of herself, but she also had a new sense of strength. Whatever the new feeling was that was coming over was delicious, and on hearing her describe it, I knew she was experiencing the lifting of the depression.

Armed with this experience she next faced her mother, and the same emotional reactions followed. From her mother she transferred this technique to the grocer. Not

98

getting a good cut of meat one day, she took it back and insisted on another cut worth the money she had spent for it. And so it went. The mouse in her had died and so had the blues. Ruth was never the same after that. In addition to this new-found self-respect, she saw a marked change in the degree of respect she now received from others. They no longer automatically told her what she was to do, they asked most politely. And if Ruth was able to do the favor, she did so gladly. If not, she refused it and that was that. The smile on her face, the lilt in her step, and the lively look on her face clearly indicated that the doormat was talking back.

If you are a doormat or a mouse, then think over very carefully why you can't stand rejection, and think over very carefully whether your standing up for yourself causes people their disturbances. Unless you see these two pieces of nonsense for what they are, you will never break free and be yourself. The result will be abuse, contempt, and dominance by others, and depression for yourself.

When to Give In

Since self-pity is often a matter of giving in too constantly to others, the question naturally arises, "When should I give in and when should I stand my ground?"

The answer is fairly simple. Give in on issues that matter very little to you. Stand your ground on issues that matter a great deal. Sometimes you may be able to live with a compromise and sometimes you may not be able to do so. Follow your feelings in this respect.

The only weakness in this advice is in the difficulty most people have of deciding what is really important. I suppose the best way to gauge this is to ask yourself whether you can lump the frustration gracefully or whether you will find yourself becoming more and more bitter about giving in until you finally have to explode.

Martha hated to make an issue with her husband about his being tardy when she waited to pick him up after work. He often let her wait far beyond any reasonable time she thought he would really need. But because she didn't want to make waves she didn't say anything and have a big hairy scene. So she tolerated her husband's thoughtlessness for months, all the while getting more and more peeved, until one day she blistered the poor fellow's ears so badly he was absolutely speechless. She felt so bad over this loss of control that she apologized the next day and went right back to waiting for him while he loitered and she sat. No longer did she feel she had a right to make an issue, because, after all, what is so awful about having to wait thirty to sixty minutes for your husband if it keeps peace in the family and keeps the marriage together?

Martha would have been so much smarter to recognize her true feelings: she detested waiting and felt that her husband had no reason whatever for dillydallying in the shop while she was sitting out in the hot sun or the freezing winter. The number of depressions she could have spared herself are countless. All she had to do was realize that she was irritated by this unthinking behavior and even though she could ignore it for a while she was sure to say something about it in the long run. And that was the key to her making up her mind. If she thought she could not indefinitely keep her mouth shut about his behavior, then the sooner she spoke up about it the better. At least that way he would know immediately where he stood; she would feel better immediately because she had gotten her gripe off her chest; and lastly, because the gripe was registered early enough it would never become a vicious attack.

Martha could have had one more powwow with her husband, warned him that she would drive off if he were not out in the car after five minutes past closing time, and then do precisely that. In no more than one or two instances would he have clearly seen how important this issue was to his wife and he probably would have hopped to. It is what we do about what we say we will do that counts, not what we say we will do. Or, to be trite, actions speak louder than words, and no more is this true than in this sort of situation.

Let us review this matter once more. Waiting for a late husband may not be a big thing with you, but it was for Martha. Therefore, it was her obligation to herself, and to her husband, to do something about it. She, furthermore, knew it was more than merely a passing annoyance by the fact that she could not overlook it. If she could not overlook it, she should then deal with it, and the sooner the better. For her, waiting in the car was, therefore, not something she should have given in to. She might not have minded it if her husband had stepped out on her; in that case she could have accepted his running around philosophically. Another woman might not have accepted that with tranquillity. So be it! To each his own. Only be true to yourself and recognize what you will tolerate and what you won't. Then either ignore it for good or do something about it the very next time it comes up.

Is Violence Ever Justified?

You may now be wondering if physical blows are included in my belief that one has a right to stand up for himself. Damned right! But only in self-defense. Hitting people (children excluded) should be limited only to those rare occasions where one might be harmed. I see no other reason for harming adults, and can also not see any good coming out of a beating under any other circumstances.

There is even a better reason for not resorting to violence. To avoid being manipulated, you need only refuse to cooperate with the person trying to control you. You do not have to sneak up on him and pound him over the head with a rolling pin while he sleeps. That kind of behavior can get you a life sentence at the most, and an excellent enemy at the very least. You are also likely to get a pounding yourself one day if you use that solution.

A better method to avoid being controlled is to refuse to cooperate with your controller. For instance, the wife of a jealous husband can allow herself to be dictated to and remain home to avoid an argument because Roger thinks she is going to hold hands with every third fellow she meets. If she does this, she will stop enjoying herself by not getting out of the house. Then she will feel sorry for herself, and presto, she is depressed.

Or, she can tell him sweetly that she is going to the bowling alley with a few of the girls. And if Roger starts shoving her around, she should fight back. He started using violence, so she has a right to fight back. However, if she weighs only 105 pounds and he weighs 180 pounds and is also a karate black belt champion, she would be a fool to defend herself that way. But she could call the police later, or she could divorce him unless he saw her right to be free and go out when she wanted. Having some time to herself and going where she wants is a right she has as an adult. If she gives in on this issue, she will make a dictator out of her husband. So she might just as well let him know in no uncertain terms what aggression is going to accomplish for the male chauvinist pig!

It may seem to some of you readers that I am taking a rather hard-nosed stand. Such is not the case. I am only suggesting that people who are controlled by others usually get their fill of it sooner or later, and if they act sooner, they spare themselves a lot of grief. I have known any number of women who for years excused their cowardice with all sorts of rationalizations: "I'd get hurt." "The children need a father." "How could I make out alone?" But when the day comes on which she cannot take his bullying any longer, all those excuses go out the window, and suddenly our sweet, cowardly, and scared rabbit of a wife finds the strength to face Mr. Mean. The sad thing about her action is the fact that it came so late. Some women don't get up enough gumption until they have suffered abuse from their children, employers, or husbands for twenty years. They don't realize that they have a breaking point, that that point will be reached someday, so why not do something about it early and avoid years of suffering?

Only Lions Love Martyrs

One of the last things I want to say about self-pity is that it often backfires and turns people *against* you whom you so desperately want *for* you. The truth of the matter is that the world hates a martyr. This is the last attitude the martyr wants, since he is so sold on the notion that his suffering has just got to touch the heartstrings of those close to him. It touches their strings all right, but not in the heart. It is the nerves that get touched, because the martyr is trying to act aggressively even though he denies it. But the person for whom the martyrdom is being played senses clearly that he is being attacked. That is precisely why martyrs are not popular anymore, and it probably accounts for the reason why they were fed to the lions two thousand years ago. We wouldn't tolerate such inhumane treatment today, but what we do to the martyr today is sometimes almost as unkind. We give in to him. This encourages him to be more self-pitying because he has been rewarded for his tear-jerking performance.

If you don't believe that long-suffering people are disliked for their display of pain, then just look at how easily people pass by beggars. There the poor devils sit, in rain and in sunshine, crippled legs tucked up under half-empty trousered legs, or blind eyes staring into a black sky, and all they want is for you to buy a pencil from them. A nickel from every passerby would give them some of the amenities of life. But how often have you seen even every fifth person give a beggar a coin? Not very often, I'll wager. And why not? Because the poor fellow counts on you and me feeling so guilty for not being in the shape he is in that we look away. Or we don't give him alms, because we think he is using his infirmity to squeeze a dime out of us. Unfortunately people are turned off by self-pitiers, even where their justification for feeling sorry for themselves is enormous. Imagine how much less pity you will get from your friend or your spouse over the trivial things you want him to pity you for. If people will pass you by even though you are blind and lame, how do you expect a positive reaction from them when all you have to complain about is the fact that you haven't been to the movies in two weeks?

Self-pitiers of the world, stop it! You are using a

method of control that works only on the stupid and weak and that makes a first-class sap out of you also. There are better ways of getting what you want out of life—for example, standing up for yourself, not worrying about how many people love you, accepting things as they are if you can't change them, not building events out of proportion or believing you must have your way at all times and will die if you are frustrated. Make those changes in your life and I guarantee you that there will be far less self-pity in your life and far less depression as well.

5

Poor You!

WE NOW COME TO THE THIRD AND LAST MAJOR REASON for psychological depression other-pity. This has its problems with learning now attitudes, as I will show you. In this instance, however, you will find yourself feeling guilty for *not* taking too seriously the problems that others have.

Just as it is perfectly possible to get depressed and gloomy by pitying yourself, there is no reason whatever that you shouldn't become blue and moody when you pity another person. That makes sense, doesn't it? In fact, if I wanted to be sweeping about it, I could even make a point for there being only two essential causes for depression: self-blame and pity. Pity applied in any direction can depress you. Pity yourself, pity others, even pity animals or things, such as a city, a landscape, a plane. I remember being quite gloomy years ago when I had to drive my car to the junkyard. It had thrown a rod and wasn't worth fixing up. I got $30.00 for it from the junkman and was lucky at that. To understand my reaction to leaving that car, however, you should know that it was the first car I purchased all by myself, I did a great deal of work on upholstering it and painting it (even with a shaving brush), and most of all, it took me all the way from New Jersey across the Rocky Mountains and the Painted Desert to come to its final grave in cold and desolated Wyoming. As I walked out of the junkyard I turned for one last look at my beautiful friend who had been so faithful through so many trying days, and as I saw it among all those ugly wrecks, my heart almost broke. I felt sorry for my car. It didn't deserve such an end, but there wasn't anything I could do about it. I couldn't even blow taps for that brave soldier that carried me to Salt Lake and graduate school. Every once in a while I wonder what happened to my little Willys and what it looks like today.

So getting depressed about a lovely city dying, your birthplace changing over the years, or your dog being run over is all too natural a reaction and comes under the heading of other-pity.

The Fear of Being Callous

One of the biggest reasons other-pity is so common is the guilt that people feel for *not* being depressed over the misfortune of others. Not being depressed at a funeral could be understood as being rude and callous. Not getting blue strikes others as being indifferent and not caring. So people will give forth emotions not just because they really do feel upset but because they think they *should* show emotions if an unhappy event occurs. Social etiquette practically demands that certain events be accompanied by very specific emotions. A mouse in a room full of people has got to get the women screaming. It wouldn't be normal if they didn't scream even if there was no way in the world for the mouse to get up the lady's leg. If they all wore slacks and their pants legs were tucked into ski socks, the women wouldn't think

108

of not screaming. The situation simply demands this stereotyped behavior.

It is particularly difficult not to respond to situations where compassion is expected. To be calm about pain or personal loss is often viewed as cruel and uncaring. It need be neither, but to show calmness and lack of intense emotion simply gives people the impression that we don't care about the person's plight.

What would you think of someone who aided his friend into an ambulance because of a broken leg but then immediately returned to the softball game? Sounds hard, doesn't it? Yet, if the fellow saw to it that everything possible was done for his friend, if he was sure that the friend's parents were notified and that they would be receiving their son at the hospital, then wouldn't it seem reasonable that he had done all he could and might he not just as well return to his game and have fun? I suppose that still strikes you as unfeeling, but only because you have been taught to think of caring for others always in terms of how upset you get. People find it difficult to believe that undemonstrative people can truly feel intensely or that well-adjusted people can put tragedy out of their minds without treating the tragedy as a trifle.

The Irrational Ideas That Cause Other-pity

Depending on how you look at it, there are one or two irrational ideas that create other-pity. The first is that unhappiness is externally caused, that we are made disturbed by others, and that our emotions have nothing to do with the way we view things. The second is that one should be upset and disturbed over other people's problems and disturbances.

Unhappiness is not externally caused, but frustrations frequently are. What happens to our frustrations usually depends upon us—whether or not we will be disturbed. If we challenge vigorously the idea that frustrations at point A need to upset us at point C, we will eventually get to the point where we will be able to think our way out of feeling blue over another person's miseries. Practically any experience can be accepted with serenity if one works at thinking rationally about it. People have faced the firing squad, terminal cancer, starvation, all without having a psychotic depression.

So, the next time you see a starving infant on your television screen remember that what you saw was most regrettable but not capable of disturbing you unless you let it. And if you see a live starved infant, you needn't get depressed either, unless you allow yourself to. Instead of having a nervous breakdown over a starving infant, wrap him up in a blanket, give him some food, and get him to a hospital posthaste.

The second idea behind other-pity is simply that you think you ought to get upset because others are upset or are in trouble. Now why in heaven's name *should* you be? Does your suffering help the victim? Are you more able to be of assistance because you have gone and upset yourself mightily over his problems? If so, how? Do you mean to tell me that you wouldn't know how to help someone unless you first worked yourself up into a lather? If so, then why are we being told all the time to keep cool, not to lose our heads, and that easy does it? But no, we still usually get excited, flustered, and depressed first, and then, after we have had a minor neurotic reaction, decide we had better do something. Isn't that a waste of time and energy? How much better our performance would be if we could really size up a predicament quickly, keep our cool, and swing into action even though we are dealing with a tragedy, and thereby truly be of efficient assistance.

This is not too often the sequence unless the person has had considerable experience with tragedy. Rescue workers, medics in the Armed Forces, physicians—all are persons trained in dealing with humans in great distress without falling apart. In fact, we count on their keeping their wits about them and wouldn't have anything to do with them if they couldn't separate the other party's suffering from their own. In their training they are watched for this trait, the ability to have compassion without excessive sympathy, to show concern without being overly concerned. If they cannot demonstrate this, they will not get far in their training. This ability to stand apart from suffering would be impossible unless these professionals actually agreed on the ideas that unhappiness is not externally caused, and that they didn't have to get depressed or upset because the people they are helping are depressed or upset.

Concern vs. Overconcern

Any civilized person has feeling for the sufferings of his fellowman. The fellow who does not have empathy or sensitivity for what people go through is obviously neurotic, moronic, or a jerk. Caring for the plight of one's fellowman is the hallmark of civilized man. But caring too much is not. That is the important line you must draw if you want to stay healthy.

"How do I know when I'm caring too much instead of just caring?" you may ask. Simple. When you hurt. When you start getting depressed and gloomy or angry, that is when you are caring too much for the other person and

111

that is when you are acting neurotically. Yes, neurotically, because your hurt is only adding misery to his misery. What your friend wanted from you was not for you to be pained and depressed. He expected you to pull *him* up to your level of cheerfulness, not let him pull you down to his level of despair.

A perfect example of how other-pity seems perfectly noble but was really very harmful and ineffectual was the case of a social worker who saw me about her depressions. I quickly determined that she couldn't take the sorrow she saw every day as she went on her rounds of the ghetto. After returning home to her comfortable apartment in the evening, she would think about all the misery she had seen that day, and the weight of other people's burdens became so great that she couldn't eat. Eventually she became more and more listless, until some days she couldn't even return to her work. Our conversation was something like this.

"Ms. Angelo, you've got to stop caring so much for those people you want to help or you won't get over this depression. The thing that's really depressing you is your belief that you *should* be upset and disturbed over other people's problems and disturbances."

"Yes, that's it exactly. I do think I should be upset for those poor children, those dirty apartments where there's no sunshine, and where the adults can only sit around all day and go crazy. It breaks my heart to see that day after day."

"*It* does not break your heart, Ms. Angelo. *You* break it. You keep telling yourself that you *should* be disturbed, that their problems have *got* to upset you, and that you have no control of your emotions in this situation whatever. If you would think those nutty ideas over very carefully and stop believing you had to be upset over

112

others' problems, I guarantee you your blues would lift overnight."

"But how am I supposed to just push that stuff out of my mind? I see misery day in and day out. I just can't go home and forget it," was her protesting reply.

"I'm glad to hear you can't forget what you see during the day, for otherwise you'd be very callous and I'd suggest you needed therapy to give you a sense of human feeling for your fellowman. But honestly, Ms. Angelo, do you have to care so much that you get disturbed? If you really believed you didn't need to be upset, would you be?"

"No, I suppose not. But how can I possibly convince myself that I can look at that poor human condition every day and not get depressed?"

"By thinking through your neurotic ideas very thoroughly and asking yourself if they make sense. First, you know from what I've told you before that you upset yourself; things can't. Secondly, since you're busted up because of all the misery you see in the world, what can you do to relieve it? Do you dig in and clean up an apartment? Do you go down to city hall and raise a ruckus? Do you even write a letter to your congressman, or a letter to your newspaper?"

"No, I am sorry to say I haven't. But I see your point. Instead of getting depressed, I should get mad."

"I prefer the word 'indignant.' You should protest, fight, raise your voice, get some action going. That might change conditions in the slums. But instead, being the sweet person you are who gets all bent out of shape because of the poverty she sees all day, you go home and add to the misery you're complaining about. How smart is that and how much do those people who need your help appreciate that? You feel so much for their problems

113

that you get sick and can't get back to work the next day to help them. Who needs that?"

Fortunately, Ms. Angelo could quickly see how foolish and unnecessary her behavior and symptoms were. She stuck out her chin, stopped being an emotional dishrag, and seldom missed a day's work thereafter.

Another example of how wasteful and even dangerous other-pity is came to me through a kindly old gentleman, a Mr. Wall. He read a great deal and knew a lot about politics. The thing that steamed him up was crooked politics and how it took advantage of the little business-man. His brother was shafted by petty local politics, and this hurt Mr. Wall so much that he became restless, couldn't sleep, and was one bitter fellow. The worst part of it was the fact that he had a very bad heart and it didn't do him any good at all to work up a sweat over the trillions of injustices in this world. But Mr. Wall identified so closely with the underdogs and felt so deeply for the hurt they experienced in this unfair world that he almost burst even while he was telling me about it. He got red in the face, his breath was labored, and he perspired as he told me about injustice and suffering in the world. It scared me as he went on, because I could envision him having a cardiac arrest right there in the office. Finally, to quiet him down I screamed over his voice and reassured him that I too knew the world was a stinking place but that we both had better get used to the smell. I praised him for his concern for his fellow-man but also pointed out that his having a heart attack and bleeding psychologically was not the solution his disadvantaged friends were hoping for. What had he done about crooked politics? Had he run for a political office himself, or helped someone campaign, or stuffed envelopes at an election headquarters?

114

He had done none of these, so we debated for a time on the utter stupidity of his nearly killing himself over conditions he did nothing to relieve aside from shooting off his mouth. Eventually he learned to accept ugly reality more gracefully, although at his age and in his condition he could not actively correct or contribute to the causes he honored. The depression and the agitation lifted nicely and when I last heard from him he was still alive. I hope that he didn't get himself worked up too much over the problems and disturbances of others and die of a heart attack.

In both of these examples, it is simple to see how healthy and kindly concern for the welfare of others was converted unwittingly into marked depression in one case, and almost death in the other. Overconcern, not concern, was the culprit. Each of these fine individuals could easily have detected when they began caring too much: the moment they realized they were upset they could also have realized they were being neurotic and self-defeating.

Emotional Blackmail

One of the most serious consequences of pitying others is the malicious use to which that human weakness can be put. For instance, if I know you have the tendency to feel excessive sympathy for me, that puts me in a position of control should I want to use it. Just imagine what I can get away with. I can make you invite me to your home, I can make you marry whomever I choose, and I can make you work in whatever occupation I think best. How much more control does anyone need? If I can do all that, then I have your soul also. Does this

115

sound farfetched? Then listen to this: I can't tell you how many people have told me that they married their spouses because he or she threatened suicide. How many parents have gotten their children to live at home far into adulthood just so they wouldn't be alone? Haven't you ever been controlled because someone used your own guilt feelings to make you give in to him? Practically everybody has used this technique and has had it used upon himself. It often works beautifully simply because you have the complete cooperation of the person you want to control.

Don't let the suffering of others turn you away from what you consider your best interests. If you feel strongly about marrying Roger and your dad goes into a depression over this prospect, don't give up your fiancé to please dad or you will be accepting his emotional blackmail.

There are several terribly important facts to remember if you want to avoid being emotionally blackmailed. First, no matter how upset the other person gets over your behavior or your plans, do not blame yourself for his disturbances. Your father, or whoever is blackmailing you, is upsetting himself. Tell him so. Offer to take him to the nearest clinical psychologist so that the poor fellow can stop his self-pitying. If he gets insulted at this suggestion, then drop the matter and go about your business while he goes about his.

Secondly, when the blackmailer tries to tell you he is doing all this for love of you, don't believe him. The blackmailer hasn't any real desire to let you be an independent human at all. He will be happy only when he gets his way. So he is hoping to make you so uncomfortable with his tears, moaning, and anxiety that you will take pity on his poor soul and give him his way. He

116

is really interested almost exclusively in his own ends, not in yours.

Thirdly, don't let someone's threat of suicide get you down. If he uses that weapon on you, tell him instantly that you refuse to be responsible for his death, that he has control over his life, that the whole idea is a stinking trick, and that if it makes him happy to die, then go to it. This is not as callous as it sounds. To do otherwise is perhaps to induce the person to try suicide in the hope of getting you to give in. But if you make it crystal clear that you regret his taking such an action while at the same time you grant him the freedom to take it, you may be amazed at how this nonsense stops. Only recently I heard of another case of a daughter whose father threatened to kill himself numerous times in order to manipulate his family. One fine day the daughter answered the phone. Good old dad made the same threat, but this time daughter took a deep sigh and candidly told her father that if that is what he really wanted to do, to go ahead. He never threatened his family again.

Fourthly, pitying others weakens them. Instead of bolstering up their courage, as you think you are doing, your sentimentality is merely telling them how much of a schnook you think they are and how you fully understand why they should be depressed. The individual already is telling himself: "Poor me. I'm too inadequate to deal with this issue." And you come along with your other-pity and in effect say to him, "Poor you, you really are too inadequate to handle this issue." How in the world is the self-pitier supposed to get stronger through that treatment? Obviously he can't.

One young boy who was brought to me because of his excessive timidity was the unwitting victim of his mother's great feeling for him. He was one of the most protected children I had ever seen. His well-meaning mother wouldn't allow him to try bike-riding when all the other boys were learning to ride, because Mike was supposedly "too uncoordinated." By the same token Mike didn't attempt swimming, roller skating, or softball until the other fellows were quite accomplished at these sports.

At first Mike protested, but his mother worried so much over him that the poor chap began to soak up her pity for him to the point where he lost his natural youthful adventuresomeness and spontaneity. Instead, Mike wouldn't risk a thing if it could conceivably hurt him.

Happily his mother was truly a caring and intelligent person and could follow my reasoning quickly. I instructed her to stop the pity and to let the boy take his chances. Instead of her turning the color of a white sheet when he wanted to go swimming with his buddies, I ordered her to control her anxiety for her son, put on a brave and cheery smile, and send him forth with a pat on the rump. Sure he might drown, I agreed, but what was happening to him anyway? Wasn't he slowly dying of boredom and excessive safety? Life is a gamble and there is nothing you or I can do about removing all its dangers. Mike's mother tried to spare her son some of those hardships and dangers, but in reality she placed him in the greatest danger of all: not being able to face new situations, not developing the proper skills whereby he might be able to avoid danger, not developing in him a sense of self-assurance which is far better than a lonely corner. Sure, he might get his shins skinned or his leg broken, but so what? A broken leg can heal easily in a matter of four to six weeks, but a broken spirit may take a lifetime to mend.

Mike's mother did her homework well. She didn't give

118

the usual clues to him which always signaled her concern, and this gave him new courage. She didn't twist her handkerchief, bite her lip, shed tears, tighten up, or ask a lot of questions implying that he was walking into death's jaws every time he wanted to cross two streets to go to a candy store.

At first the mother simply forced herself to let her son go and it nearly made a depressive out of her. For a time I thought I was going to have to give her individual appointments for *her* emotional problem. As Mike became more and more of a normal boy, however, and as he became slightly aggressive and occasionally acted like a brat, she relaxed as she saw his new strength. He learned to ride better, to swim as well as the next boy, and to play a decent game of ball. The few minor injuries he suffered were fortunately not so bad as to make her go back on her new strategy. Luck frequently plays a bigger role in our emotional lives and in our whole development than we realize.

Other-pity Can Frequently Cause a Legal Injustice

Justice often calls for stiff measures. Being soft when you should be firm can cause all sorts of unfairness. And what causes more sloppy sentimentality than other-pity? Nothing! Getting gushy and soft about another person can cause you to misunderstand him completely and to treat him in ways not really in his own best interests.

Take the case of Mr. Polin. He drank too much, always drove when he drank, and had racked up a list of accidents while under the influence of alcohol. None of this seriously interfered with his drinking, however, because he simply continued to be careless about his behavior and not to realize the danger in which he placed others.

119

One night he narrowly missed hitting a pedestrian, but he did smash up a parked car.

Among the jurors was one of my clients, a Ms. Clark, whose major psychological problem was other-pity. I had worked with her on this problem for several months and she was in excellent control of this tendency when she was asked to sit on the jury.

On the day the jury retired, Ms. Clark had a most interesting experience. She found herself completely alone in wanting to find Mr. Polin guilty as charged and deserving a heavy fine plus a short jail sentence. She had no pity for the defendant and believed a good spanking might make him grow up and act responsibly. The rest of the jury, however, wanted to soft-pedal Mr. Polin's accident and let him off very easy in view of the little damage actually caused to the car in question. This did not satisfy my client, because she was far more concerned about the need to make a solid impression on Mr. Polin than about the need to judge him solely on this one incident.

She said: "It occurred to me that the entire jury was suffering from other-pity just as I had done all my life. I knew the signs well and could just see the wheels going around in their heads. They were probably telling themselves that he was a nice guy and didn't mean to run into that car; that he would surely learn by this experience despite the fact that he had done this sort of thing before; and that they'd feel badly if they caused him to lose money or spend time in jail. Well, as you know, doctor, I've been there and I know how feeling sorry for someone else can foul you up good, even to the point where you are being hurt by not learning the right lessons.

"This whole jury was surprised and shocked at my insistence that we make this guy see his behavior for what

120

it was. They wanted me to give in to them, but I wouldn't. And don't you know, after several hours of debating the case I had them all won over to my side. And best of all, I believe they felt good about their decision, because they could focus on the good they were eventually doing him rather than the immediate relief he would have gotten. They overcame their other-pity and could deal with this problem quite easily, just as I did."

Ms. Clark had good reason to speak so knowingly. Part of her difficulty as a mother was her inability to be firm with her children because of the temporary frustration her restrictions would cause them. So, instead of insisting that they study, she let them go out and play in the evenings. Instead of making sure that they practiced their instruments, she let their early musical interests wane and disappear. Instead of making them clean up their rooms and help around the house, she did the work herself. She pitied them whenever she expected work or responsibility from them. They sensed that she was an easy mark for a long face, so they put on the "poor me" act and got her to back down on practically every one of her rules. In the end they wound up spoiled and unmanageable brats whom she had trouble liking.

This was a serious injustice to her children. Her pity for them made her weak and stupid. They ran the house and loused up their lives as a result. When she went into court, she could sense how this drama was being reenacted, but this time she was prepared for a mature, firm reaction rather than a whimpering, pitying reaction, and she was prepared to do that man a service by being tough on him even if she had to take an unpopular stand with the rest of the jury.

An immense amount of injustice is committed in the name of love. It is time to redefine the word "love" and expand it into something that includes the idea of caring for someone beyond the immediate moment, for what is satisfying now is often bad for us in the near future. Other-pity only considers the current frustration, not the frustrations that lie months and years ahead.

Other-pitiers Raise Self-pitiers

Of all the faults with other-pity, none is so damaging as the creation of self-pitiers. To see this, all you have to do is watch a mother and a child in a park. The child falls and hurts himself, but he tries to bear up against the pain. His mother has not seen what happened because she is reading a book. Her son then comes up to her, a pained expression on his face, holding his kneecap where it was skinned. At the moment of realization her heart melts for her boy, she cuddles him in her arms, holds him tight, makes a catastrophe of the skinned knee, and signals to him that he ought to cry because he has to be in awful pain. And that is precisely what the child then does: he pities himself and *then* breaks into howling sobs. When this scene is enacted often enough, the end result has to be one thing and one thing only: a self-pitier of the first order.

If the mother would curb her maternal enthusiasm, recognize her son's accident, even tell him that it must hurt and that he is free to cry if he wants to, and then wash the wound off with her handkerchief, she will have shown him an entirely different way of responding to such mishaps. She will have been caring and compassionate without being gushy and pitying. Nothing in this last description could hurt her son. It could only help him. But there is a great deal in the former method that might stunt his growth.

The simple truth of the matter is that self-pity comes easily enough to human beings, but when it is backed with maternal or paternal love, watch out! Once a family of children get the "poor you" treatment for a few years, they soak up that nonsense so thoroughly that they can't think of others any longer, only of themselves.

One of the sorriest cases of other-pity backfiring which I had ever encountered was that of Ms. Bee. She was one of those good mothers, always sacrificing for her children and husband, going without just so they could have, and being glad of the opportunity to serve. All her feelings were so completely invested in her family they truly began to believe that the world revolved around them, that mother was there to serve them, and that they had a positive right to be highly indignant if they didn't get their cotton-picking ways. So her husband began to go out with the boys because he enjoyed it. When she kindly asked to be taken along sometimes or to be dined on the weekends he felt so put upon that she felt guilty for asking.

Though she worked for pin money for a few extra-nice clothes for herself, she always wound up getting something new for her whining daughters who thought that their mother owed them a new wardrobe every season. After a while they helped less and less with the housework, and even her asking for her husband's help to make the girls mind didn't have the desired effect. When she reached the point where she could clearly see that she had become a maid and personal servant she still could not express her wrath but instead pitied herself and phoned me about her thoughts of suicide.

My advice to her was clear and simple. "Stop feeling for that crew of yours. Make them toe the mark. Stand up to them. Let them scream like stuck pigs if they want to, but don't give in on any pretext."

Alas, the advice was simple enough but impossible for this well-trained martyr to follow. All it took was one firm, "No!" from her husband, and an indignant exit from the room by her daughters and she was a defeated creature once more. She didn't see me again, but I can clearly guess that the pattern at home is the same and that she will continue to be depressed from other-pity and self-pity.

"If It Hadn't Been for You"

A very common way others seduce you into feeling sorry for them is to place the blame for their disturbances on you. Then you are supposed to see what a heel you have been and do an about-face by giving your accuser everything he wants.

A young wife came to me once, very much depressed because of the great guilt she felt over upsetting her husband frequently, and over the remorse she felt for him as a result of her mistakes. This at first sounded as though she had a good deal of insight into her marriage, but in order to be sure I questioned her.

"Ms. Schafer, can you give me an example of what you are referring to?"

"Certainly, doctor," was her reply. "Last week the police came to my house asking for my husband. They had a warrant for his arrest for car theft. They claimed that the car my husband bought last week was really stolen. I was shocked, of course, and simply couldn't believe it. But it was true, all right. He told me he had purchased it and he made up a big lie about how much it had cost and how he had financed it, and if I didn't believe him, I could go to the savings book and see a withdrawal last week for the amount of the down payment. When the police and I both put him on the spot, he insisted he had stolen it because I made him do it."

"You made him steal a car?" I asked.

"That's what he insisted. It seems I expressed a desire for a new car recently and then he insisted that if it hadn't been for me asking for a new car, he wouldn't have been compelled to go out and steal one. He says I'm always making him do things he doesn't want to do. And I guess he's right. After all, if I didn't make the requests in the first place, he wouldn't have reason to steal things for me when he cannot afford them. When he put it this way I felt so guilty for being so selfish and inconsiderate, and I felt so sorry for the burdens and pressures I put on my husband."

It was quite apparent from her weird tale that her ever-loving hubby was a sly old fox and really had a live one in his trap. I used to marvel when I heard such ridiculous accounts, but I don't anymore. Now I nearly throw up at the utter gullibility of some people. Can anyone actually believe that she *meant* every word she told me? Scout's honor, she did indeed!

I was able to help her wake up by showing her first of all that she cannot make someone steal anything unless she puts a gun to his head and threatens to blow his brains out unless he steals. And even then she can't make him do it if he really doesn't want to, because he can always decide to die rather than live under those conditions. Secondly, I pointed out that her husband was a spineless wonder or he would have had the nerve to tell her he didn't have the money for a car. He could have told himself that having his wife think poorly of him would have been unpleasant but hardly catastrophic. Had he done so he could easily have allowed her innocent comment to go in one ear and out the other.

That sly old fox didn't do that, however, because he had too much neurotic pride to admit he wasn't a magician or a millionaire. In view of these faults which he clearly possessed it was easy to pose the logical question, "Now, Ms. Schafer, how can you blame yourself for actions for which your husband was clearly responsible?"

"I think I can follow you so far, doctor, but what about his argument that none of that would have happened if I hadn't expressed a desire for a new car? You must admit that all of this probably would not have happened if I hadn't made the request in the first place. Right?"

"Right," I agreed. "Perhaps none of this would have happened if you hadn't made the suggestion to have a new car. However, just because you did make the suggestion does not mean you are responsible for what followed. You have an indirect share of the responsibility, I agree, because you did make the request. But if that's true, then there are a whole host of people who should also share in the guilt for this act and feel sorry for what they're doing to your poor husband."

"Like whom?"

"Like the car manufacturer for making such lovely cars. And like the company he works for because they don't pay him enough to buy expensive cars when he wants them. And like the social system we live in that says we must pay for things we want. Aren't all these parties also indirectly guilty for your husband's act? But would you seriously hold them responsible and say they made him steal?"

The debate went on for the remainder of the therapy session, but as we drew to a close she could begin to see my reasoning and see her husband's antics for what they were. In time she could see him as a weak fellow, very

126

eager to have his wife's love and foolish enough to do almost anything to assure himself of her respect, but also as someone who was too defensive to see his own behavior clearly and who then played on the sympathies of others by making them feel guilty over an innocent act while at the same time feeling much sympathy for him.

Learn this lesson early in your life and you will be spared a great deal of grief: no one can make you do anything unless by force. People do what they do because they want to or because they are afraid to turn you down because they want your approval so badly. Either way, that is something they are responsible for. So never let them blame you or make you feel sorry for them when they have voluntarily committed a folly.

6

Some Final Advice

IF YOU HAVE FOLLOWED ME DILIGENTLY THUS FAR, YOU will have been exposed to the latest and soundest thinking on the subject of depression. Many of you will show surprising improvement in your emotional lives simply because you are the kind of person who profits by reading. Some people are that way. Others, however, may be stimulated by this theory but not be able to use this new knowledge on themselves to any great degree. They will need to counsel with someone in order to bring these words to life and to give them personal meaning with regard to their own problems. And some people have behavior patterns so deeply ingrained that no book would ever be able to break them of their bad habits. To these last two groups I dedicate this last chapter. In these final pages I want to advise you how to seek out a competent therapist, suggest some of the best books for you to read for a broader understanding of human behavior, and wind up by giving you several important comments about depression in general.

Don't Choose Your Therapist Blindly

There can be a world of difference between one therapist and another. I am referring not only to the obvious differences one would expect between one personality and another. I am referring also to the enormous differences between how one person conducts psychotherapy and how another does. Most people do not realize that there are many schools of thought in psychotherapy and that we therapists most emphatically do not agree with each other as to who is doing good or bad therapy. So beware! Ask your therapist what his theoretical orientation is before you decide to spill your psychological beans to him.

If he tells you that he is a Freudian, you can expect him to take a long time with your problems, to sit in silence a great deal and let you do almost all the talking, and to explore your childhood with you because he believes that that is the basis of all current psychological difficulties. Furthermore, he will analyze your dreams, your feelings toward him, and your feelings toward any other person who was important to you. You will not necessarily be psychoanalyzed, because that form of therapy has been modified so much that it has become a rarity. Freud and his followers thought nothing of seeing clients each day for five or six days a week and kept up this marathon for years. Today, if you see a Freudian therapist, you will find that most likely he will not even use a couch, he will face you directly and carry on a normal conversation, but his theory otherwise will not have changed much. For instance, he still believes that therapy should provide the client with an emotional ex-

130

perience, not a set of new ideas per se. He will be working toward getting you to face the upsetting events of your past and then try to get you to relive them with him in his office. By reexperiencing them as an adult, you will be more aware of how you behaved over the years and why. More important, however, is the fact that you will be seeing these emotions as an adult and will not need to react to them with anger or fear as you might have as a child.

Personally, I regard psychoanalysis as old-fashioned and not worth your time or money. It was a valuable tool to investigate the unconscious with, but it does not hold wide acceptance outside of psychiatry as a method of treatment.

If the counselor you are thinking of getting therapy from tells you that he is a Rogerian, expect him to be a very accepting fellow, someone who will not criticize you, who will not dispute anything you tell him, and who will at times sound like your echo. He will take practically everything you say and, with a little twist, say it back to you so that you cannot help feeling that he understands you completely. He does this in the belief that as you feel more and more comfortable to open up in his presence, you will get deeper and deeper insights until you can draw all the conclusions you need to settle your emotions.

I have found this method to be helpful at times when a client was afraid he would be scolded or pounced upon. By simply showing him that all his thoughts and feelings are completely understood, he cannot help feeling at ease. The major fault with this system, however, is that no advice is given to the client. Anything he learns from therapy he must arrive at by himself under the soft touch of the therapist who kindly urges him to look further and further into himself. This will, of course, work at times, but I feel that the same results could often come more quickly by simply telling him what the therapist thinks and openly advising him as much as he wants.

Or you might find yourself in the office of a behavior modification therapist. These are psychologists or psychiatrists who follow the work of Pavlov, the Russian who conditioned dogs to salivate to the sound of a bell. This is an excellent method to use for certain fears or phobias and may require you to be hooked up to a small electric shock machine. For example, you may be told that each time you feel afraid, you are to give yourself a small shock on your hand with a pocket shocker, which you would be asked to buy.

The theory behind behavior modification is that we have learned our behaviors, even our neurotic behavior. Someone rewarded us for being angry, depressed, or fearful and if we now get a small electrical jolt each time we have these emotions, they will become extinguished.

Instead of using the shock method, the therapist might ask you to imagine all the things you fear. When you can do that, the therapist (who has previously relaxed you completely by getting you to tense your muscles first and then relax them) asks you to imagine your doing the next item on your list, and so on up until you can think of the worst fear without getting anxious.

Behavior modification is still so new as a clinical tool that we are not sure how to use it in many mental health centers or private practices. Its applications will doubtlessly expand in time and it should be carefully watched as it grows.

You could wind up in the office of someone who calls

himself an eclectic and this means that he is not particularly partial to any major school of psychotherapy. He
takes the best from each system and uses it in his own
unique way. At times he may seem like a follower of
Freud, then of Rogers, then sound like a rational-emotive
therapist, and so on.

There is certainly nothing wrong with this, because in
the hands of a good therapist the eclectic approach lends
versatility and ingenuity to therapy. Actually, I believe
that every good therapist should be somewhat eclectic.
After all, all the schools of therapy have something to
contribute and should be honored for their contributions.
Yet, I call myself a rational-emotive therapist despite the
fact that I am also eclectic. I do this because so much
more of my goal and method is strictly RET that I might
as well label myself that as anything else.

The major point I want to make is that you cannot be
sure that the therapist you are considering is a rational-
emotive therapist unless you inquire. If what I have offered in this book interests you and you want further
counseling along these lines, you almost certainly must
connect yourself with a therapist who believes that
changing attitudes is the proper therapeutic goal. If you
cannot be sure of this matter but feel comfortable with
the therapist, it is reasonably safe to give that person
a try. Just believing in RET is not a magic powder that
makes a good therapist. Some rational-emotive therapists
are undoubtedly poor therapists. So, if you have a choice
between two therapists you respect and one follows the
RET persuasion, choose him. If you must choose between two therapists, neither of whom is acquainted
with RET, choose the one you feel most comfortable
with, or who has the best reputation.

One more thing to watch out for: judge for yourself whether or not the therapist you have in mind is mature and mentally healthy or not. If he has some of the same problems you have, forget him. Do not expect much help with your poor self-discipline from a therapist who has a sloppy desk and who cannot get his work done, or who is obese. These fellows need as much help as you do. Or if you know of a therapist who frequently flies off the handle or who gets depressed, forget it. He won't do you much good either. Your therapist, though not God, should certainly be pretty good at what you want from him. Just as you wouldn't want guitar lessons from someone who played only slightly better than you, you also wouldn't want to be counseled by someone whose own house isn't in order.

Differences Between Psychologists and Psychiatrists

When choosing a therapist, you may be confused over the issue of whether to seek out a psychologist, a psychiatrist, a minister, or a psychiatric social worker. Because the major confusion is over the first two I will focus on their separate backgrounds and talents.

The clinical psychologist, if he has a Ph.D. (doctor of philosophy degree) in psychology, has had four years of graduate education in psychology and related fields. His education is quite broad, and underlying it is the assumption that he must be trained as a scientist who can add to the knowledge he has learned at school. Also, as a psychologist, he has all behavior, human or animal, as his proper area of study. The clinical psychologist has a year of internship experience to complete during which time his clinical work is supervised.

In the practice of clinical psychology the psychologist

serves the public through his psychotherapy, his psychological testing, and his research efforts.

The psychiatrist, on the other hand, is an M.D. (medical doctor) who specializes in abnormal behavior just as some physicians specialize in surgery, dermatology, or obstetrics. When a physician decides to specialize in psychiatry he receives three additional years of residency experience.

In his private practice the psychiatrist often counsels clients just as the psychologist does, or as the psychiatric social worker and the minister do. But he also administers drugs, gives electric shock sometimes in his office but more often in a psychiatric ward of the local hospital.

These are the major differences between these two professions. When you have to decide which profession to entrust yourself to, consider two questions: Do you need medication, shock, or hospitalization? If so, see a psychiatrist. Do you want only counseling? If so, choose your therapist on the basis of his skill and reputation and the school of therapy he practices. Being a psychiatrist does not make a man a good therapist. I have known social workers who were better therapists than some psychologists or psychiatrists I have known. The decision of which therapist to work with should not be a matter of his discipline but of his personality and theoretical persuasion.

If you need personality, intelligence, or vocational studies made, you should seek out a psychologist: a clinical psychologist, that is. We have educational psychologists, industrial psychologists, experimental psychologists, developmental psychologists, and so on. They will not do you and your emotional problems much good, because abnormal behavior is not their field. That area is the concern of the clinical psychologist.

135

Worthwhile Reading

I have touched on only one big emotional problem: depression. For those of you who want to know more about other emotional disturbances and how you might deal with them in others—your children or your friends—the following books are recommended:

The Rational Management of Children, Second Edition, by Paul A. Hauck. Libra Publishers, Inc., 1972.

Getting children started on the right foot requires knowledge as well as love. The best-intentioned parents can wind up doing a very bad job of raising children simply because they never learned to understand their children and to control their own emotions. In this book I attempt to pass on to parents the major findings from my own experience as well as the contributions of other thinkers regarding child-rearing.

How to Live with a Neurotic, by Albert Ellis. Crown Publishers, 1957.

This book is a real gem. The helpful suggestions and insights that Dr. Ellis gives about living around annoying family members and co-workers are worth rereading many times. The great number of instances when his words become applicable to those other people in our lives is surprising. Even years after having read his book the first time I still find new applications of his unique thinking. This is a must for everyone concerned about the quality of his social life. It is especially geared to those with a taste for reading but with limited exposure to psychological terms and a limited education.

A Guide to Rational Living, by Albert Ellis and Robert A. Harper. Prentice-Hall, Inc., 1961.

The more sophisticated reader will enjoy this book

immensely. Drs. Ellis and Harper have written a masterpiece in the field of self-help books. This is one of those volumes which therapists refer to clients all across the country because it reads so well, humorously, yet professionally. It deals with a wide spectrum of emotional disturbances and explains the theory of rational-emotive therapy as well. If you are one of those persons capable of benefiting from what you read, get this book!

Growth Through Reason, by Albert Ellis. Science and Behavior Books, Inc., 1971.

If you want to learn what rational-emotive therapy actually sounds like and what takes place during a typical RET hour, this is the best book to illustrate that. Five contributors from around the country present a total of eight verbatim cases, generally starting with the first or one of the early sessions in therapy, and winding up with a word-by-word transcript of the final hour. Dr. Ellis makes running comments about each therapist's session, and this too is quite instructive.

This book is the next best thing to being in therapy yourself.

Reason in Pastoral Counseling, by Paul A. Hauck. The Westminster Press, 1972.

Although the title suggests that only ministers might enjoy this book, actually there is a great deal the average person can find in it if he is interested in the relationship between psychology and religion. Since so many people think that the two are incompatible, and that a person must either follow his religious teachings or follow the latest psychological findings, but not both, I felt compelled to show ministers and intelligent laymen where this was not so. As I have shown in the book you are now reading a new view about guilt and depression, so in *Reason in Pastoral Counseling* I have shown the harmony between psychology and religion with respect to hate and fear also.

A Few Final Tips

1. Your depression will end even if you do nothing about it. So don't despair when you get blue. Sunshine is just over the horizon! That is one of the few fortunate features about depression which we cannot report about anger, for instance, or about fear. It is possible to be timid, fearful, shy, and anxious for practically the whole of one's life. And it is perfectly possible to be resentful, bitter, hateful, or angry for practically every day of one's life. But when you have an episode of depression you can count on one thing for sure: whether you take medicine for it or not, it will end; whether you receive counseling for it or not, it will end; and if you do nothing about it, the depression will end. So why get counseling? To shorten the duration of the depressive episode, to reduce the severity of the episode, and to prevent future episodes.

No matter how blue and gloomy you may feel at times, try to remember that this feeling of despair will someday be history. Count on it. You don't have to kill yourself to get over your blues, all you need is patience!

2. The thoughts I have conveyed to you in this book are sound and will help anyone suffering from psychological depression. I personally have had fantastic success in helping some people for whom, before I formulated this theory of depression, I would have had to cross my fingers and hope that I could do them some good. Now I don't do that because I know that I am on the right track and that my formulation of the RET principles with respect to depression are correct and bring on

138

results. If the reading of this book doesn't do you much good, don't blame me, it is your fault. Either you didn't study the material well enough, you didn't apply it seriously enough, or you need personal counseling and can't be helped only with the written word. Whatever the reason, the fault lies not in these ideas. They have relieved some of the most stubborn depressions I have encountered in my practice.

3. Don't be afraid of counseling. Many people dread the thought of getting into counseling, presumably because they will discover all sorts of dreadful things about themselves. On the contrary, most people begin to learn a few beautiful things about themselves. They learn that they are really pretty decent people. They learn that they have a right to forgive themselves for whatever wrong they commit. They learn how to get over hate, fear, self-blame. They learn to be more at ease with themselves and not always dependent on others.

They learn this and much more. So why should they shirk such a beautiful experience? Because of the old bugaboo about mental illness. Too many people still think that talking to a "shrink" proves they have lost their minds and they must take every precaution not to let their spouses and friends know they are seeing someone professionally. How stupid! When you stop and realize that practically everyone could use the services of a psychotherapist one or more times during his life, that all of us are neurotic quite frequently (and that includes me too), then why in heaven's name should the rational and mature person feel embarrassed about getting psychotherapy? It is the person who does not see a "head shrinker" when he is upset who ought to have his head examined.

It is easy to get over any embarrassment about getting

into counseling if you will view it as you would a school subject. The name of the course could be "The Personal Dynamics of John Doe" or "The Intimate Emotional Life of Sarah Jane." You go to class about once a week, report to your instructor what success or failures you had in practicing the advice he gave you last week, and you get more advice and instruction. The whole experience is normally a beautiful one, filled with wonderful new insights, and great in its effects on you. One sweet young thing I counseled once expressed it best: "Before coming to see you I thought there was some big, black, and ugly thing inside me, and I was afraid that counseling would make me face it. Now that our counseling is over I can see how perfectly ridiculous that was, because now I can see that there never was such a creature at all."

4. "Should I take counseling for depression if I am on medicine for it also?" This is a question sometimes posed to me and I answer it as follows: If your depression or disturbance is so great that you require medicine, then by all means take your tranquilizer or energizer. Follow your physician's directions carefully. But don't think for one moment that medicine is going to teach you what caused you to become upset or that it can teach you how to calm yourself. Only your thinking can do that. If the medicine helps you think more calmly, well and good. The ultimate goal, however, for a sane and healthy life is not to be well stocked on medicine, but to keep calm and reasonably happy without medicine. This can be done only if you start learning the ABC's of emotional life. Then, and only then, can you use your head as one great big tranquilizing pill. That, in the final analysis, is the best medicine you have. Use it. You will surely find that the more thinking control you gain over your emotions the less medical control you will resort to.

140

There you have it, dear reader. Thank you for staying with me this far. I hope you have enjoyed the visit and will come back often. And each time you come back to these pages I trust that you will have brought yourself just a little bit farther up from the blues.